# RANCH RAISED

## COOKBOOK

## HOMEGROWN RECIPES
## FROM OUR FAMILY TO YOURS

**MARY HEFFERNAN**

*with Kim Laidlaw*

PHOTOGRAPHY BY CHARITY BURGGRAAF AND KATHRYN GAMBLE

SASQUATCH BOOKS
SEATTLE

TO MY STRONG, LOYAL, HARDWORKING HUSBAND,
who appreciates every hot meal I put on the table, and
to my four little Marys, who inspire me to keep cooking
*Ranch Raised* recipes daily.

# Contents

# FIVE O'CLOCK COCKTAILS
## 213

# SOMETHING SWEET
## 229

# The Five Marys Story

**I**n 2013 our lives took an unexpected turn. My husband, Brian, and I had a comfortable lifestyle in Silicon Valley with our four healthy girls, great jobs, and a beautiful home. We worked hard to make a good living there for many years: Brian owned his own small law firm, and I had built a number of small brick-and-mortar businesses, including two restaurants. We had lots of great friends and many social commitments. We had everything we were supposed to want—we were living the American dream. But we were inspired to change the direction of our lives. We bought a ranch and decided to move to a rural mountain town to raise livestock together as a family.

I grew up in Menlo Park, the heart of Silicon Valley, before it became a bustling hub of opportunity. I left California to attend college in Virginia, where I started on the path to medical school. After college, I returned to my hometown and started tutoring local kids. I saw a need for a place where the kids could do their homework with tutors on staff, so I started my first business, called Academic Trainers. It made me realize how much I loved owning a small business. And I had big ideas for more.

A few years later I was volunteering at a fundraiser and met a tall, handsome guy who drove a pickup truck but spent his days in a suit and tie. It was love at first sight. Brian was working his way up in a big firm, and I was managing my tutoring business and working on my next venture. We were married in 2006. After our first baby, Francie, came along, Brian decided to start his own law practice and leased office space upstairs from my business.

We enjoyed working close to each other and decided we wanted more of that. Along with a few other family-centered businesses, we opened two farm-to-table restaurants serving quality food made from the best ingredients we could find. We worked with top local chefs to identify just what we wanted and what was important to us.

Sourcing consistent, high-quality meats year-round proved to be difficult. After a lot of research and a few years of searching, we knew exactly what we were looking for: well-marbled Black Angus beef from cattle with excellent genetics that were raised naturally on grasses and finished with barley. We wanted beef that was dry-aged for twenty-one to twenty-eight days for outstanding flavor and consistency every time.

When we couldn't find anything that met our criteria, we decided to do it ourselves. We found the historic Sharps Gulch Ranch in the mountains of Northern California outside of Siskiyou County—or we like to say it found *us*. Our hope was that we could build an operation to produce our own consistently excellent, humanely raised meats, all while continuing life as we knew it.

With some help from my brother-in-law, a fifth-generation cattle rancher in Eastern Oregon, we set up operations and jumped into ranch life while trying to run our businesses in Silicon Valley. When we purchased the property, we thought we'd just go up on the weekends, hiring a ranch manager to handle

the day-to-day operations while we managed our businesses during the week. We quickly realized we couldn't do both things well.

A few months later—and about two hours into the six-hour commute we made every weekend—I turned to Brian and asked, "What are we doing? Driving to the ranch every weekend is not sustainable. Let's commit to this full time." It was an easy decision to make. But it wasn't easy to unwind the life we'd created.

Brian and I decided to sell our home and all of our businesses, including our two restaurants and his law firm, and move our family of six to the ranch for good. It was a huge change. We left behind the only livelihood we'd ever known and set our sights on creating a life and a sustainable business in a rural town with a population of just 681 people.

This decision wasn't much of a shock to those who knew us. People often ask my mom if she's shocked we ended up as ranchers, and her answer is always "No, it makes perfect sense for Mary and Brian." Brian and I both have deep roots in California agriculture and share a love of the rural Western lifestyle. In 1867 Brian's great-great-grandfather Casper and his wife, Theresa, came to Ventura County from Germany to farm sugar beets. Casper was known as one of the first agriculturalists in the region. The couple eventually bought the four-thousand-acre Conejo ranch. Their son, Antone, continued ranching and later settled in Orange County, where Brian's dad started their family in agriculture. Brian's dad, Tom, was a banker in Ventura as a young man but decided to go back to his farming roots when Brian was an infant. Moving his young family to Imperial County, Tom grew alfalfa, grains, and specialty crops. When Brian was sixteen, the family moved north to Tehama County, where Tom began to farm prunes, almonds, and walnuts. Sadly, he suffered greatly from Parkinson's soon after the move and passed away in 2015, but Brian's dad made many visits to our ranch before he died. He was clearly very proud to see his son following in his footsteps.

My ancestors immigrated to the Pajaro Valley from Ireland in 1851 and grew strawberries, apples, lettuce, and sugar beets in Santa Cruz County. They sold gold-rush supplies to miners and worked as farmers in the Watsonville area for five generations. Much of my family remains in California to this day. My grandfather moved away from farming but was a great man with big ideas and an entrepreneurial spirit. He always appreciated farmers and ranchers and found his own business niches—a trait I like to believe he passed on to me when I was a young girl riding around in the front seat of his car while he talked about his next big idea.

So Brian and I set our sights on creating a new business in ranching in the mountains of Northern California. We had a big job: we needed to find a way to make the ranch work to support our family, and possibly even support the

next generation someday. The first year of business was tough—Brian and I jumped with both feet into a life we hardly knew. We had 1,800 acres of pastureland and mountain hillside, and quickly started growing our herd of cattle, flock of sheep, and passel of pigs.

It took us well over a year to determine the best way to ship and sell the meat we were working so hard to produce. We raise the animals for market, meaning that we breed and care for them before harvest, and then after butchery we ship the beef, pork, and lamb directly to customers all over the country. Little by little we grew our business from the bottom up, selling small boxes to friends and family, traveling for deliveries, and selling from farm stands. Eventually we opened the Farm Store, from where we now ship our meats directly to customers' doorsteps anywhere in the United States.

Moving to the ranch was a big change for our home life as well. All of a sudden our family went from sharing a spacious house in the suburbs to a rustic 760-square-foot cabin with only a wood-burning stove for heat. Our initial thought was to live in the cabin for a short time while we got our bearings and eventually build a larger house on the property. But we soon realized we craved the comfort of the cabin; we all loved being so close together. We simply didn't need much more space. We spend so much of our time outside working that this small, cozy home is perfect for our family and all that we need.

Living on the ranch has made our four daughters—ages seven to twelve and all of whom really are named Mary—extremely independent and resourceful. We honestly couldn't do all this without them. The hard, physical work of raising animals, growing hay, and running our businesses has meant we've relied on them to help from the very beginning. The girls were young when we moved to the ranch, but we quickly realized that they were so much more capable than we could have ever imagined. They learned how to drive the hay truck, take care of their horses, and are in charge of the bottle babies, helping the momma animals through difficult births.

This collaborative effort has allowed us to branch out beyond livestock. Not long after moving, we built our camp area up the hill from the cabin so that we'd have a place to host family and friends on the ranch. We also offer summer experiences, where we share the food we raise, cocktails, and a little more about ranch life and what goes into raising animals with our guests.

In 2017 we opened Five Marys Burgerhouse, a restaurant and bar in town, after swearing we'd never open another restaurant. But when the opportunity to purchase the historic bar came up, it just made sense. We serve all our own meats to the local community as well as to guests who visit from near and far. We also produce our own small-batch single-barrel whiskey with our partner

Alchemy Distillery in Arcata, California, and use local produce raised by our neighbors whenever possible.

Taking a chance by purchasing the ranch and jumping in with our family was the best decision that Brian and I have ever made. We look back at where we were just a year ago, or six years ago, when we started from scratch and can't believe how far we've come. It hasn't been easy, but as we like to say, "Nothing is easy—if it were, everyone would do it. But it's worth it."

This cookbook is a culmination of all of this, an invitation to join us around the table to share a meal, a glimpse into our free-range life of dirt and sunshine and animals and community. Because, at the end of the day, when the sheep are tucked away in the barn and the woodstove is warming the cabin, there's nothing we like more than to gather in the kitchen, cooking together and savoring some of our favorite family recipes. We are proud to share them here with you, and we hope you enjoy sharing them with your own friends and family.

*Mary*

MaryFrances (Francie) is twelve and has a natural confidence and beauty about her. A leader in our family, she is fiercely loyal and can often be found with her nose in a book or saddling up her horse.

Francie

MaryMarjorie (Maisie) is maternal and takes great care of her sisters, and can also handle just about anything on the ranch. She was the first sister to learn to drive the tractor and operates a stick shift better than I can.

Maisie

MaryJane (Janie) is a pistol and keeps us all laughing with her dry sense of humor. She is opinionated and loves to go on hiking adventures in the mountains with her dad.

*Janie*

MaryTeresa (Tess) was only fifteen months old when we bought the ranch. She's now a seven-year-old barefoot, piggy-loving, bottle-baby-feeding, horse-riding, mutton-busting ranch girl through and through.

*Tess*

Ranch
Breakfasts

**B**RIAN STARTS HIS DAY AT 4:45 every morning. When the weather is cooler, he makes a fire in the woodstove to warm up our house and sits nearby with his coffee and laptop to make a plan. At first light, he pulls on his hefty work boots, grabs his Stanley mug, and heads out to feed the animals.

There's a beauty and quiet in that predawn stillness that I love, in the house and everywhere around the ranch. The girls are still tucked up in their loft and the cabin is warm and cozy. Often, though, one, two, or all four of the girls will layer up and jump on the feed truck with us and head out to the pastures for early-morning chores.

The first priority is to feed the cattle, pigs, and sheep, and the girls know the rule in our family is the animals eat first and we eat second. After the first round of chores are finished, and the girls get ready for school, I have a little down-time to get in the kitchen and cook for the crew. Having enough fuel to get through a busy day is always important. Sometimes Brian works through lunch, so he might not eat again until dinner—on these days, a big "ranchers" breakfast is essential.

I might make cast-iron baked eggs and sausages in spicy tomato sauce or a veggie-rich frittata and thick-sliced toast slathered with homemade butter. Other days, I put out a basket of warm biscuits with homemade jam and a plate piled high with crispy bacon or Five Marys sausages. Special mornings call for waffles or Dutch baby pancakes, especially when either of our moms is visiting!

After breakfast, it's off to school or back out for more chores: fixing a fence or collecting chicken eggs from the barn, corralling escaped sheep (a.k.a. "Momma's Damn Sheep") or tending to the newborn animals. Regardless of what it involves—because there's always something unexpected that comes up daily—we've got the energy to tackle another full day on the ranch.

DURING THE SUMMER UP AT CAMP, especially during retreat weekends, we make breakfast sandwiches with our homemade English muffins, piling them high with scrambled or fried eggs, cheese, and crispy bacon or sausage patties. When we want to up our game, we make this egg sandwich with plenty of garlicky aioli, thick slices of ripe tomatoes from the garden, smoky ham or our favorite sausage, peppery arugula, melted cheese, and an over-medium farm egg. If you like, swap in crusty sourdough toast or a biscuit for the homemade muffins, but they are definitely worth the effort.

# FRIED EGG, TOMATO, AND ARUGULA SANDWICHES <u>WITH</u> GARLIC AIOLI

*Makes 6 servings*

To make the aioli, in a small bowl using the back of a teaspoon, smash together the garlic and salt until a paste forms. Whisk in the mayonnaise, lemon juice, and oil until well combined. Set aside or refrigerate until ready to use, up to 2 days.

In a large nonstick skillet over medium heat, melt the butter. Crack the eggs into the pan, leaving space between each one and trying not to break the yolks; you'll probably have to do this in two batches. Sprinkle with salt and plenty of pepper. For sunny side up, cover and cook until the whites are opaque and the yolks are slightly runny, about 4 minutes. For over-medium (or over-hard), flip the eggs after 3 minutes and cook to the preferred doneness.

Meanwhile, toast the muffins until golden. In a second skillet over medium heat, warm the ham for about 30 seconds.

To assemble, spread the cut sides of the muffins with a thin layer of aioli. Divide the meat among the bottom halves of the muffins. Top each with a slice of cheese, an egg, a slice of tomato, and some arugula, in that order. Cover with the top halves and serve at once.

**FOR THE AIOLI**
1 small clove garlic, minced
⅛ teaspoon kosher salt
½ cup mayonnaise
1 teaspoon freshly squeezed lemon juice
1 teaspoon extra-virgin olive oil

**FOR THE SANDWICHES**
2 tablespoons unsalted butter
6 large eggs
Kosher salt and freshly ground black pepper
6 large English muffins, homemade (page 33) or store-bought, split
6 to 8 ounces sliced ham, 6 cooked thick-cut slices bacon, or 6 cooked sausage patties
6 (1-ounce) slices cheddar cheese
6 thick slices ripe tomato, preferably heirloom
1½ cups baby arugula

THIS IS ONE OF MY FAVORITE breakfast dishes, especially when we have guests up at Camp. It's beautiful cooked in a cast-iron skillet and served hot right from the pan. Instead of links, you can use loose sausage; just brown it in a skillet, then add it back to the tomato mixture. I like to keep toppings like fresh herbs, sliced avocado, sour cream, and jalapeño slices on the side so we can garnish each portion to everyone's tastes.

# BAKED EGGS WITH TOMATOES, SAUSAGE, AND FARMER CHEESE

*Makes 4 to 6 servings*

Preheat the oven to 400 degrees F. In a 12-inch heavy ovenproof skillet over medium heat, warm 1 tablespoon of the oil. Add the sausages and cook, turning every so often, until nicely browned all over and just cooked through, about 6 minutes. Transfer to a cutting board.

Add the remaining 1 tablespoon oil, the potatoes, and onion to the skillet and cook, stirring occasionally, until the potatoes start to brown, about 7 minutes. Add the bell pepper and cook, stirring occasionally, until the vegetables are tender and nicely browned, about 7 more minutes. (If the potatoes are taking a while to become tender, cover the pan for a few minutes to help speed them along. Reduce the heat slightly if the vegetables start to get too brown.) Stir in the garlic with a pinch of salt and cook just until fragrant, about 30 seconds.

Add the canned tomatoes with juices, paprika, another pinch of salt, and a few grinds of pepper, stirring to combine and scrape up any browned bits from the pan. Bring the mixture to a gentle boil, then reduce the heat to a simmer until it thickens and becomes fragrant, about 5 minutes.

Cut the sausages into ½-inch slices and add them to the skillet. Continue to cook, stirring, until the mixture is bubbling and warmed through. (If it looks a little dry, add a few tablespoons of water; you want it to resemble a thick, saucy stew.)

Using the back of a large spoon, create eight wells in the tomato mixture. Crack an egg into each well and season with salt and pepper. Transfer the pan to the oven and bake until the egg whites are barely cooked and the yolks are still runny, about 12 minutes. (The eggs will continue to cook out of the oven.)

Top with dollops of farmer cheese, the green onions, and cilantro. Serve right away with crusty bread.

2 tablespoons extra-virgin olive oil, divided

¾ pound lamb merguez or Italian sausage links (about 4 links)

1 pound Yukon Gold potatoes (about 2 potatoes), cut into ½-inch chunks

1 small red onion, finely chopped

1 red bell pepper, chopped

3 cloves garlic, minced

Kosher salt and freshly ground black pepper

1 (28-ounce) can diced fire-roasted tomatoes

1 teaspoon sweet paprika

8 large eggs

½ cup farmer cheese or crumbled feta

2 green onions (white and green parts), thinly sliced, for garnish

½ cup chopped fresh cilantro leaves or flat-leaf parsley leaves, for garnish

Crusty bread, for serving

# FREE-RANGE CHICKENS

We have lots of chickens who free-range on the ranch, enjoying the dirt and sunshine all day and foraging in the grass. They work to keep the ranch tidy, picking up the scraps of food the pigs leave behind in their troughs, finding bugs in the pastures, and cleaning up the grain hay left behind when we feed the sheep or the cows. They roost high up in the rafters of the old barn, safe from predators, and lay eggs in the nesting boxes, where the girls scramble in after school to collect the eggs in old metal baskets. When we first moved to the ranch, Brian and I built a little roadside stand, where we sold the eggs by the dozen, but when we opened the restaurant, we decided to use the eggs for our customers. There we fry them up for our signature egg-topped burger or whip the protein-rich orange yolks with bacon and jalapeños for our deviled eggs. And the difference in flavor, color, and freshness between our free-range ranch eggs and store-bought is significant!

BRIAN'S ALL-TIME FAVORITE BREAKFAST IS a hearty egg-potato-and-meat burrito. We typically use leftover meats like sausage, brisket, pulled pork, or even ground beef. I love using our farm-fresh eggs because the flavor is so much richer than store-bought. Whenever possible, I recommend buying pasture-raised eggs directly from a farmer, at roadside stands or from farmers' markets. Adding sautéed peppers and onions gives these great color and flavor, and you can easily adapt this recipe with whatever leftovers you might have on hand. Brian likes to devour his often-overstuffed break-fast burrito with plenty of vinegary hot sauce, like Frank's RedHot or my garden chili sauces, plus a side of sour cream.

# BREAKFAST BURRITOS

*Makes 6 to 8 burritos*

In a large well-seasoned cast-iron or nonstick skillet over medium heat, fry the bacon, stirring, until it is crisp and the fat has ren-dered, 5 to 10 minutes. Use a slotted spoon to transfer to paper towels. Pour out all but about 1 tablespoon grease, then add the potatoes, bell peppers, and onion to the skillet. Cook, covered and stirring occasionally, until the potatoes are tender, 10 to 13 minutes.

While the vegetables cook, preheat the oven to 175 degrees F. In another skillet over medium-high heat, warm the tortillas. Wrap them in aluminum foil and place in the oven to keep warm.

In a large bowl, whisk together the eggs, milk, a few dashes of hot sauce, and the spice rub (or salt and pepper) until combined. When the potatoes are tender, season them with salt and pepper, then stir. Reduce the heat to medium-low and add the egg mixture and reserved bacon to the skillet. Cook, stirring occasionally, until the eggs are cooked through to your liking.

Lay the warm tortillas out. Divide the cheese among the tortillas, spreading it in an even layer in the center of each. Top the cheese with a big spoonful of the egg mixture. Add a few dashes hot sauce, then top with a few avocado slices. Fold in two sides of each tortilla, then roll up burrito-style. Serve at once with hot sauce, salsa, and sour cream on the side.

½ pound thick-cut smoked bacon, roughly chopped, or bulk breakfast sausage

¾ pound russet potatoes, diced

2 small red or orange bell peppers, quartered and thinly sliced crosswise

1 small white or yellow onion, halved and thinly sliced

6 to 8 (10- to 12-inch) flour tortillas

10 large eggs

¼ cup whole milk

Hot pepper sauce and/or salsa

Generous pinch of M5 Spice Rub (see page 127; optional)

Kosher salt and freshly ground black pepper

1½ cups (4 ounces) shredded pepper Jack or cheddar cheese

1½ ripe avocados, halved and sliced

Sour cream, for serving (optional)

THE WHOLE FAMILY LOVES THESE big, fluffy biscuits with plenty of butter and drizzles of our sticky-sweet Five Marys golden honey. When I have fresh strawberries in the fridge—especially if they are past their best days—I'll whip up some jam to smear on the biscuits right when they come out of the oven. This is my girls' favorite way to enjoy them. For a heartier breakfast that will see you through all your morning chores, split the biscuits and top them with creamy sausage gravy (see page 110)—always a big favorite of Brian's.

# BUTTERMILK BISCUITS WITH STRAWBERRY–LEMON JAM

*Makes 6 large biscuits and 2 half-pints jam*

To make the jam, place a small plate in the freezer to chill. In a medium heavy saucepan over medium-high heat, stir together the strawberries, sugar, and lemon juice. Bring to a full boil, then reduce the heat to medium and boil gently, uncovered and stirring occasionally, until the berries become very tender and the juices thicken, about 20 minutes. Watch the jam and reduce the heat as needed so it doesn't boil over or burn. The jam is ready when a small amount firms up slightly when spooned onto the frozen plate. Use a potato masher to mash up the berries if you like, then set aside to cool completely. To store, transfer the jam to clean airtight containers (such as 2 half-pint jars), and refrigerate for up to 1 month or freeze for up to 3 months.

To make the biscuits, preheat the oven to 425 degrees F. Line a large rimmed baking sheet with parchment paper.

In a food processor, pulse the flour, baking powder, salt, and baking soda to combine. Add the butter and pulse until the mixture resembles coarse bread crumbs. Add the buttermilk and pulse until the mixture just comes together.

Turn the dough out onto a lightly floured work surface. Gently press the dough together, then fold it over itself a couple of times. Press the dough into a ¾-inch-thick disk. Use a 3¼-inch biscuit cutter to cut out as many rounds as possible, pressing straight down and not twisting the cutter. Transfer the biscuits to the baking sheet, spacing them 1 inch apart. Press together the dough scraps and cut out the rest of the biscuits; discard the remaining trimmings. You should have 6 biscuits.

Bake until golden brown, about 15 minutes. Serve the biscuits warm with plenty of butter and jam.

**FOR THE JAM**
1 pound ripe strawberries, hulled and chopped
⅔ cup sugar
3 tablespoons freshly squeezed lemon juice

**FOR THE BISCUITS**
2 cups all-purpose flour
1 tablespoon baking powder
1 teaspoon kosher salt
½ teaspoon baking soda
6 tablespoons cold unsalted butter, cut into small pieces
1 cup plus 2 tablespoons well-shaken buttermilk

# SWEET AS HONEY

We love having bees on the ranch. Not only do they help pollinate the gardens and grasses grown throughout the valley, but we get to harvest our own honey a few times a year. We have a colony of beehives out on the pasture by the river. Our local bee-keeper manages the hives and collects the honey with his able crew so we can share the bounty with our customers. The bees feast mostly on our ranch-grown alfalfa—which blooms into beautiful purple flowers—along with wildflowers and clover. You can taste the natural environment in the finished product: unprocessed raw honey straight from the source. One of our specialties is our spun honey, also known as whipped or creamed honey. It's so sweet and creamy in texture, it tastes almost like frosting, but it's totally natural with no additives. My girls like it by the spoonful straight out of the jar or spread onto homemade biscuits or English muffins with butter and cinnamon. And I love adding honey to a charcuterie board alongside soft, strong blue cheeses and salty prosciutto or salami—it's heavenly!

MAKING YOUR OWN SAUSAGE IS easy and gives you a chance to find your favorite combination of spices and just the right amount of sweetness. It also gives you control over the quality and variety of ingredients. Always start with premium, fatty ground pork, nothing too lean (look for 80/20 or even 75/25), and then experiment with seasonings—such as minced fresh rosemary or a Mexican spice blend—to make it just the way you and your family like it best. I sometimes make bigger sausage patties and load them onto homemade biscuits (page 27) or English muffins (page 33) with an egg for a hearty breakfast that gets us ready for a productive day.

# BREAKFAST SAUSAGE WITH FENNEL AND SAGE

*Makes 4 to 6 servings*

Preheat the oven to 200 degrees F and place a baking sheet in the oven on the center rack.

In a medium bowl, whisk together the sugar and all the spices. Add the pork and mix with your hands until everything is well combined. Divide the mixture into 12 equal portions (about 2 ounces each) and press into ½-inch-thick patties about 3 inches in diameter. Transfer to a platter.

Heat the oil in a large cast-iron skillet over medium-high heat. Add half the sausage patties and cook until well browned on the bottom, 2 or 3 minutes. Turn, pressing down on the patties with a silicone spatula to thin them out a little, and cook until cooked through and browned on the second side, about 2 minutes more. If the pork isn't fatty enough, add a little more oil during cooking. Transfer the sausages to the warm baking sheet in the oven while you cook the remaining patties. Serve at once.

3 teaspoons packed light brown sugar (optional)

2 teaspoons dried sage, or 1 tablespoon packed minced fresh sage

1½ teaspoons kosher salt

1 teaspoon fennel seeds, or ½ teaspoon ground fennel

½ teaspoon dried thyme, or 1 teaspoon packed minced fresh thyme

½ teaspoon garlic powder

½ teaspoon red pepper flakes

½ teaspoon freshly ground black pepper

1½ pounds ground pork

1 tablespoon canola oil, plus more if needed

THESE ENGLISH MUFFINS ARE ALWAYS worth the extra time it takes to make and proof the dough. It's become a signature dish for breakfast at Camp. In fact, our guests usually make them regularly at home after trying them with us! If you've never had a homemade English muffin, there's nothing like it. The tangy buttermilk is the secret ingredient. We make our muffins on a big cast-iron griddle right on the stovetop, and everyone gathers round to help—most don't know you cook them on a griddle! I like to serve them up as a breakfast sandwich heaped with scrambled eggs, cheese, and chopped fresh chives, but we also love a good fried egg sandwich (page 21). Make sure you fork-split the muffins to make the most of all those bubbles in the dough.

# HOMEMADE ENGLISH MUFFINS

*Makes 12 muffins*

In a small saucepan over low heat, warm the buttermilk and water to lukewarm (105 to 115 degrees F) on an instant-read thermometer. Pour the mixture into the bowl of a stand mixer fitted with a bread hook. Whisk in the sugar and yeast, and let stand for 10 minutes to activate the yeast.

Add the flour and salt and mix on low speed until combined, about 1 minute. With the mixer running, add the butter 1 tablespoon at a time. Increase to medium speed and knead until the dough is well combined and becomes soft and springy, about 8 minutes. The dough will be quite soft and a little sticky, but it should clear the sides of the bowl. (Alternatively, you can mix the ingredients together by hand and then knead the dough on a lightly floured work surface.)

Spray a large bowl with cooking spray and add the dough, then cover with plastic wrap or a damp kitchen towel and set in a warm, draft-free place (a turned-off oven is great) until the dough doubles in size, about 1 hour.

Punch down the dough in the bowl, cover again, and refrigerate for at least 30 minutes or up to overnight. If the dough is refrigerated for more than about 3 hours, remove it from the refrigerator about 30 minutes before proceeding.

Turn the dough out onto a lightly floured work surface and roll into a ½-inch-thick round. Use a 3½-inch round biscuit cutter to cut out as many rounds as possible. Press together the dough scraps, reroll, and cut out as many rounds as possible. You should end up with 12 dough rounds.

1¾ cups well-shaken buttermilk
½ cup water
¼ cup sugar
1½ tablespoons (2 packets) active dry yeast
4 cups bread flour (about 1½ pounds total)
1 tablespoon kosher salt
6 tablespoons unsalted butter, at cool room temperature
Coarse cornmeal, for dusting
About 2 tablespoons canola oil, for brushing

➡

Dust two rimmed baking sheets with a thin layer of cornmeal and add the dough rounds, spacing them at least 1 inch apart. Cover loosely with a damp kitchen towel and let rise in a warm spot until they are doubled in height and spongy, about 25 minutes. (The total time depends on how hot or cold the room is.)

When the muffins are ready, preheat the oven to 250 degrees F. Heat two large cast-iron pans or a large cast-iron griddle over medium-high heat until warm. Brush each pan evenly with about 1 tablespoon oil, then reduce the heat to medium-low.

Gently place as many of the muffins as will fit in the hot pans, being careful not to deflate them. Cook until golden brown on the first side, then carefully turn and brown the other side, about 15 minutes total. Adjust the heat as needed and turn and rotate the muffins as they cook to make sure they brown evenly and don't burn.

Transfer the muffins to a clean baking sheet and bake until cooked through, 10 to 15 minutes. Transfer the muffins to a wire rack and let the muffins cool completely. Use two forks to split the muffins around the "equator," pulling them apart into halves. Toast the muffins before serving. Store any leftover muffins in an airtight container at room temperature for up to 2 days, or freeze for up to 1 month.

# HOMESTEAD BUTTER

It's so easy to make your own butter, plus it's a fun activity for kids and doesn't take much time. Put 2 cups of the best-quality heavy cream you can find into the bowl of a food processor (or 1 cup into a tightly lidded pint jar if you want a workout). Process until the cream turns to whipped cream and then thickens and solidifies and the butterfat separates from the buttermilk; it should take about 5 minutes (or *shake shake shake* that jar until the same thing happens, but it will take a bit longer). Pour through a fine-mesh sieve set over a bowl, squeezing the butter to separate it from the buttermilk. You should have about 1 cup buttermilk. Transfer the buttermilk to an airtight container, add 1 teaspoon freshly squeezed lemon juice, then store it in the refrigerator for up to 5 days. Use it to make biscuits (page 27) or English muffins (page 33)!

Put the butter into a bowl, add cold water to cover, and squeeze and massage the butter with your hands to remove any lingering buttermilk. You'll need to do this three or four times until the water runs clear (this helps preserve the butter and keep it from spoiling). If you like, add ⅛ to ¼ teaspoon fine sea salt and massage it in after discarding the water. You should have about ¾ cup butter. Wrap it in waxed or parchment paper and store it in the refrigerator for up to 10 days.

WHENEVER WE VISIT MY MOM, Jannie, she makes this for breakfast, and it always reminds me of growing up at home with my own siblings, everyone fighting for their share as the hot pan came out of the oven! It's the best to enjoy right away while it's hot and fluffy. You can use just about any fruit you want—fresh cherries from our friend's farm are one of our favorites, but blackberries, blueberries, or chopped peaches are also delicious. Of course, you can forget the fruit and serve it plain with lots of melted butter and powdered sugar dusted over the top, the way Tess likes it best. Baking it in cast iron helps caramelize the crust and give it a crunchy edge.

# CAST-IRON DUTCH BABY PANCAKE WITH CHERRIES

*Makes 6 servings*

In a large bowl, whisk together the eggs, milk, 3 tablespoons of the sugar, the vanilla, lemon zest, and salt until well combined. Sift the flour into the mixture and whisk to combine. Stir in 3 tablespoons of the melted butter. Refrigerate the batter for 15 minutes.

Meanwhile, place a 10-inch cast-iron pan in the oven and preheat to 450 degrees F. Add the remaining 2 tablespoons butter and swirl around the hot pan to coat. Pour the batter into the pan and immediately sprinkle with the cherries. Sprinkle the remaining 1 tablespoon sugar over the top and pop it into the oven.

Bake until puffed and golden brown, 18 to 20 minutes (do not open the oven door). Serve at once.

4 large eggs
¾ cup whole milk
4 tablespoons sugar, divided
1 teaspoon vanilla extract
1 teaspoon finely grated lemon or orange zest (optional)
½ teaspoon kosher salt
¾ cup all-purpose flour
5 tablespoons unsalted butter, melted, divided
1 cup halved and pitted fresh cherries

BRIAN'S MOM, CLAIRE, LOVINGLY KNOWN as Oma, is the queen of waffles. When she comes to visit, she's awake before dawn, whipping up a batch of batter, then heating our old-fashioned Griswold cast-iron waffle maker on the stovetop. The girls love waking up to the sweet smell of these crispy, light-as-air treats. The topping reminds me of bananas Foster—you can add a splash of rum and serve them over ice cream as a dessert, which is a fun way to turn waffles into a celebration. Or keep it simple with butter and maple syrup and a handful of fresh berries.

# BROWN-BUTTER WAFFLES <u>WITH</u> BROWN-SUGAR BANANAS

*Makes about 14 standard-size waffles*

To make the brown-sugar bananas, in a large frying pan over medium heat, melt the butter. Add the brown sugar, cinnamon, and salt. Cook, stirring, until the sugar dissolves and the mixture bubbles, about 2 minutes. Add the sliced bananas and water and cook, stirring gently, until the mixture becomes a smooth sauce, 1 to 2 minutes. Remove from the heat.

To make the waffles, in a small frying pan or saucepan over medium heat, melt the butter, then cook, stirring occasionally, until it turns golden brown and smells toasty, about 4 minutes (make sure to watch it so it doesn't burn). Scrape the butter into a medium mixing bowl and let cool slightly.

In a large mixing bowl, whisk together the flour, brown sugar, baking powder, salt, and baking soda; set aside. To the brown butter, add the eggs, buttermilk, and vanilla and whisk until evenly combined. Pour the buttermilk mixture into the flour mixture and stir until just combined.

Preheat the oven to 200 degrees F and place a large rimmed baking sheet in the oven on the center rack. Heat the waffle iron to medium according to the manufacturer's instructions. Once heated, spray lightly with cooking spray, fill with batter, close the lid, and cook until each waffle is golden brown. Transfer the waffles to the oven to stay warm while you cook the remaining batter.

Rewarm the banana topping over medium-low heat until heated through. Serve the waffles with a generous spoonful of brown-sugar bananas.

**FOR THE BROWN-SUGAR BANANAS**
¼ cup unsalted butter
1 cup packed light brown sugar
½ teaspoon ground cinnamon
Pinch of kosher salt
4 ripe but firm bananas (about 2 pounds), peeled and cut on the diagonal into ½-inch-thick slices
2 tablespoons water

**FOR THE WAFFLES**
½ cup (1 stick) unsalted butter
2 cups all-purpose flour
2 tablespoons packed light brown sugar
2 teaspoons baking powder
1½ teaspoons kosher salt
½ teaspoon baking soda
4 large eggs
2 cups well-shaken buttermilk
2 teaspoons vanilla extract

FRITTATAS ARE A GREAT WAY to use up veggies in your fridge or from your garden that are ready to be eaten—before they end up in the chicken scrap pile. You can combine the veggies with just about any meat you'd like, your favorite cheese, and fresh herbs in whatever combination sounds good that day. One of our favorites includes breakfast sausage (page 32), mushrooms, red peppers, onion, and melted cheddar or pepper Jack cheese. I top each wedge with sliced avocado, fresh sour cream, plenty of hot sauce, and maybe a few slices of fresh jalapeño!

# CLEAN-OUT-THE-FRIDGE FRITTATA

*Makes 6 to 8 servings*

Preheat the oven to 350 degrees F. If using asparagus or broccoli, fill a small saucepan halfway with salted water and bring to a boil over medium-high heat. Add the vegetables and boil until barely crisp-tender, 30 seconds to 2 minutes. Drain and rinse under cold running water to stop cooking. If using mushrooms, greens, or peppers, cook in a skillet over medium heat with a little olive oil until crisp-tender.

In a 10-inch heavy ovenproof skillet (ideally a well-seasoned cast-iron) over medium heat, warm 1 tablespoon of the oil. Add the onion and a pinch of salt and cook, stirring occasionally, until tender, about 2 minutes. Add the cooked vegetables to the pan, along with the bacon, stir to combine, and set aside off the heat.

In a large bowl, whisk together the eggs, sour cream, herbs, ½ teaspoon salt, and a few grinds of pepper.

Add the remaining 1 tablespoon oil around the edge of the skillet. Spread the vegetables evenly over the bottom of the skillet, return to medium heat, and gently pour the egg mixture over the vegetables. Cook until the egg at the edge of the pan begins to set, about 4 minutes, running a silicone spatula along the sides to allow some of the uncooked egg to flow under the frittata.

Sprinkle the cheese evenly over the top of the frittata and transfer the skillet to the oven. Bake until the eggs are just set, about 20 minutes. Then, if you like, turn on the broiler and broil the frittata for a few minutes to brown the top. To check for doneness, cut a small slit in the center of the frittata; it should be just set.

Let the frittata stand for at least 5 minutes before cutting into wedges. Serve warm or at room temperature with sour cream, hot sauce, and/or avocado.

2 heaping cups roughly diced vegetables, such as asparagus, broccoli, mushrooms, spinach, chard, and/or bell peppers

2 tablespoons extra-virgin olive oil, divided

½ small red or yellow onion, finely chopped; 1 medium leek (white and pale green parts only), halved lengthwise, rinsed well, and sliced; or 1 large shallot, minced

Kosher salt and freshly ground black pepper

⅓ cup cooked crumbled bacon, sausage, or chopped ham (optional)

12 large eggs

½ cup sour cream, plus more for serving

1 teaspoon finely chopped fresh herbs, such as oregano, thyme, or marjoram, plus more for garnish

1 cup crumbled or shredded cheese, such as fresh goat cheese, feta, cheddar, or Jack

Hot sauce and/or sliced avocado, for serving (optional)

Bites to Share

**T**HERE'S A STRONG SENSE OF community and camaraderie in ranch work because it can be such a shared effort. Ranchers don't get weekends off, and the workday often lasts from before sunup until after sundown. Sometimes there are tasks that require extra hands, whether it's moving cattle or branding calves, and bring neighbors together to help out.

One of the best ways we can thank our neighbors for their help is to serve up sustenance that keeps everyone going or to celebrate the end of a job well done. It doesn't have to be fussy or preplanned—after a long day these friends are usually more than happy to share some good food and a cooler full of cold beers.

I like to keep a few options on hand so I'm ready on short notice to throw together a spread to share. Things like beef jerky, roasted nuts, crackers, and jars of pickled veggies all store well in the pantry. Add sliced meats, such as salami or prosciutto, a few wedges of cheese, and fresh-cut fruit, and you have an instant butcher board or "grazing table" that will feed plenty. Loaded deviled eggs and Wakefield's cheesy bread are some other family favorites that hold everyone over until dinner.

You don't have to be working on a ranch to enjoy these shared bites, though. These recipes allow you to quickly and easily lay out a variety of satisfying dishes with minimal effort. They also adapt to any occasion but are especially well suited for potlucks, picnics, and backyard barbecues. It doesn't have to be fancy, it just has to taste good.

THIS WAS MY GREAT-GRANDMOTHER ELLA Arnerich's recipe, and when I was growing up my mom always made cheesy bread for family gatherings. It is ridiculously simple, and the family history claims this started as a Depression-era appetizer because the ingredients were very affordable and easy to find. My girls *love* it, and Maisie knows how to prep and make it all on her own. The secret is old-fashioned white bread cut into squares without the crust, and serving them hot out of the oven after a little broil to crisp up the tops.

# WAKEFIELD'S CHEESY BREAD

*Makes 6 to 8 servings*

Preheat the oven to 350 degrees F.

In a small bowl, stir together the onion, Parmesan, mayonnaise, and sour cream. Trim the crusts off the bread, then cut each slice into quarters. Dollop the mayonnaise mixture evenly onto each piece. Arrange the bread on a large baking sheet.

Bake until the topping is hot and the bread is toasty, about 10 minutes, then turn on the broiler. Position the pan about 6 inches from the broiler and broil until the topping is golden brown. Serve hot.

1 small white onion, finely chopped
½ cup grated Parmesan cheese
½ cup mayonnaise
¼ cup sour cream
8 slices good-quality white or French bread

BUTCHER BOARDS ARE ONE OF my favorite ways to serve and present appetizers because you can use whatever you have on hand and make them as big and elaborate or as small and simple as you'd like. This is less an actual recipe and more suggestions and inspiration, so simply use whatever meats and accompaniments you love or have around. A board is a great place to show off a variety of cured meats, jerky, and spreads; it's also perfect for a party or a tailgate-style lunch when you have a bunch of kids running around that you need to feed. At the end of a long day, when our family is hungry and ready to eat the minute we walk in the door, this is my go-to solution.

# BUTCHER BOARDS

### HOW MUCH TO SERVE
A good rule of thumb is to serve about 2 ounces of meat per person. So, for example, if you're hosting twelve people, buy a combined total of at least 24 ounces (1½ pounds) of charcuterie. Putting cheese on the board will add texture and flavor and make it go further. Plan for 1 to 2 ounces of cheese per person. Plus any leftovers can be packed into sandwiches the next day!

### CHOOSING MEATS
For a big group, it's nice to offer a variety: aged salami, paper-thin prosciutto or jamón, and some kind of spreadable meat are a good starting point, plus whatever you know your family and guests will love. Choose quality charcuterie straight from the rancher or from a local deli or butcher whenever possible.

### CHOOSING ACCOMPANIMENTS
I like to serve both crackers and sliced baguette on my boards; you can toast or grill some of the bread to add crunch. Pickled vegetables or cornichons plus a dollop of grainy mustard pairs nicely with a lot of different types of charcuterie. A little something sweet, whether it's fresh fruit or a tangy chutney, goes especially well alongside pâtés and cheeses. And nuts are always a winner for any gathering.

### PUTTING IT ALL TOGETHER
Choose a large board or flat platter. Most cured meats are best served presliced, especially those that need to be cut very thin, like prosciutto. But you can put out a whole salami and a sharp paring knife and let guests cut their own too. Spreadable meats can go on their own small board or plate, or be placed in a small bowl or ramekin (especially nduja, which is a spreadable spicy salami, and rillettes, shredded meat preserved in fat). Serve cheeses whole with a knife nearby; serve fruits sliced so they are easy to pick up and graze on; and serve nuts toasted or candied for a little extra sweetness.

### CHOOSE THREE OR FOUR THINLY SLICED MEATS
Prosciutto, speck, or jamón serrano
Hard salami or soppressata
Mortadella
Bresaola
Beef jerky

### CHOOSE ONE OR TWO SPREADABLE MEATS
Chicken liver pâté
Country pork terrine
Nduja
Rabbit, duck, or pork rillettes

### CHOOSE AS MANY ACCOMPANIMENTS AS DESIRED
Assorted crackers and/or thinly sliced baguette
Assorted local cheeses, ideally three different types (such as hard, semi-soft, and soft)
Toasted or candied nuts, such as almonds, pecans, walnuts, and/or hazelnuts
Ripe seasonal fruit, such as thinly sliced plums, apricots, melon, pears, or apple; mixed berries; and/or quartered figs
Fruit chutney, such as plum or apricot, or jam, such as fig or nectarine
Cornichons or pickled vegetables
Grainy mustard

**WE SERVE THESE AMPED-UP APPETIZERS** at our restaurant, Five Marys Burgerhouse, and while deviled eggs might seem old-fashioned, they are one of our most popular starters. The jalapeños and bacon really take them up a notch! At the restaurant we use fresh jalapeños, but I also love the vinegary kick of pickled ones, which are called for here because they're available all year long. If you have an abundance of farm-fresh eggs, this is a delicious way to use them up.

# LOADED DEVILED EGGS

*Makes 6 to 8 servings*

Fill a large saucepan two-thirds full with water and bring to a boil over medium-high heat. Using a slotted spoon, carefully add the eggs to the boiling water. Adjust the heat if necessary, and gently boil for 13 minutes. Meanwhile, fill a large bowl with ice and cold water. When the eggs are done, use the slotted spoon to immediately transfer them to the ice water. Let cool completely, about 15 minutes.

While the eggs cool, in a skillet over medium heat, cook the bacon, stirring, until crisp, about 8 minutes. Transfer to paper towels to drain.

Peel and halve each egg lengthwise. Scoop the yolks into a medium bowl and arrange the egg white halves on a serving platter.

Add the mayonnaise, vinegar, and a few grinds of pepper to the yolks. Stir and mash the mixture with a fork until smooth and well combined. Stir in the chopped jalapeños. Scrape the mixture into a pastry bag fitted with a large plain tip and pipe evenly into the egg white halves. (Alternatively, use a spoon to fill each white.)

Top the deviled eggs with a jalapeño slice, sprinkle with the bacon and paprika, and serve at once.

12 large eggs
2 thick-cut slices smoked bacon (about 3 ounces total), finely chopped
⅓ cup mayonnaise
1 tablespoon apple cider vinegar
Freshly ground black pepper
2 tablespoons finely chopped pickled jalapeños
24 slices pickled jalapeños, for garnish
½ teaspoon sweet paprika, for garnish

# CAMP

Brian and I entertained a lot in our "old life," and when we moved to the ranch, that didn't end. We went from having friends over for backyard barbecues to inviting them to come stay with us for a weekend and help pitch in on the ranch. It offered a deeper connection when we spent mornings making breakfast together and feeding the animals, then enjoying the evening after a hard day's work.

We traded a big Craftsman home in the suburbs for a 760-square-foot cabin with a little country kitchen that had no dishwasher or large gas range. It made entertaining and cooking for a crowd a little more challenging! Rather than build a big house to accommodate our guests, we instead built an outdoor entertaining space to host friends and family and customers who wanted to experience ranch life with us—a space we now call Camp.

We broke ground in the horse pasture up the hill from our cabin. Brian and I drew up lots of ideas and designed the big kitchen and dining structure with our good friend Tyler, a chef and draftsman by trade. We wanted it to feel like camping on the ranch but with all the luxuries of home. We wanted Camp to be open and airy, with great views of the ranch and our valley, a dining room table to fit all our friends and family, and all the kitchen amenities needed to feed a crowd.

A neighbor milled local wood for the structure, including some from a big old fallen tree on our ranch that became the beautiful beams holding up the roof. Another local friend and contractor, Andy Brown, helped us erect the entire structure with his team. The whole family dug trenches to plumb real working toilets, and together we put up the cozy Montana Canvas wall tents under the oak trees. Brian even designed and welded the metal frame beds that we use in all of the tent cabins!

Today, Camp is a place we gather throughout the summer for family meals, retreats, and parties. It's a great way for people to discover a little more about what we do, be immersed in ranch life, learn cooking techniques and basic butchery, and understand how and why we raise our animals the way we do. We drink evening cocktails, take sunset rides up the mountain to our favorite vista point, create fun crafts using natural elements around the ranch, and take guests along for chores. And, of course, we eat lots of great food!

AT BRIAN'S FAMILY GATHERINGS, WE divide up meal duties and I'm usually assigned "Mary's famous bacon-jalapeño poppers" by my sister-in-law. I love the spicy, fresh kick of barely baked jalapeños (possibly my favorite ingredient!), and Brian has to walk away from the appetizer tray or he'll eat them all before anyone else can get a bite. These come out of the oven molten hot, but it doesn't stop them from being snapped up before you can blink. If you want to double the bacon—always a good idea—you can top each popper with a piece of crispy bacon when they come out of the oven.

# BACON-JALAPEÑO POPPERS

*Makes 6 to 8 servings*

In a small skillet over medium heat, fry the bacon, stirring, until crisp, about 8 minutes. Using a slotted spoon, transfer the bacon to paper towels to drain and cool.

In a medium bowl, stir together ¼ cup of the Parmesan, the bread crumbs, and the paprika. In another bowl, stir together the cream cheese, cheddar, the remaining ¼ cup Parmesan, the reserved bacon, and the green onion until well combined.

Preheat the oven to 400 degrees F. Cut the jalapeños in half lengthwise, then use a teaspoon to scoop out and discard the seeds (it's a good idea to wear gloves when doing this). Arrange the jalapeño halves on a large rimmed baking sheet.

Fill each jalapeño half with some of the cream cheese mixture. Press the filled jalapeño into the bread crumb mixture, pressing the crumbs into the cheese, then return to the baking sheet.

Place in the oven and bake until bubbling and golden brown, about 15 minutes. If you like, turn on the broiler to brown them a bit more. Let cool slightly, then serve.

2 thick-cut slices smoked bacon (about 3 ounces total), finely chopped

½ cup grated Parmesan cheese, divided

¼ cup dried fine bread crumbs

½ teaspoon smoked paprika

8 ounces cream cheese, at room temperature

½ cup packed shredded cheddar or Jack cheese, or a combination

1 green onion (white and green parts), finely chopped

12 medium jalapeños

THIS CREAMY DIP SERVED ALONGSIDE a platter of sliced veggies from the garden makes for a beautiful spread with just the right savory kick. The hint of sweetness in the dip makes it a hit with the kids. In fact, it's Janie's favorite and she'll often request it if Brian and I are planning a night out with friends. She's also been known to whip up a batch herself for an after-school snack with carrots and potato chips.

# CARAMELIZED ONION DIP <u>WITH</u> GARDEN VEGETABLES

*Makes 6 to 8 servings*

To make the dip, in a large frying pan over medium heat, melt the butter. Add the onions and a big pinch of salt, stirring to combine. Cover the pan and cook, stirring every so often, until the onions are golden brown and softened, about 25 minutes. If they start to brown too quickly, reduce the heat. Add the balsamic and sugar and continue to cook, uncovered and stirring occasionally, until the mixture is well browned and sticky, about 3 minutes. Remove from the heat and set aside to cool completely.

In a medium mixing bowl, beat the cream cheese and sour cream with an electric mixer until smooth and well combined, about 2 minutes. Add the cooled onions, mayonnaise, Worcestershire, and onion and garlic powders, and stir to combine. Season with salt and pepper as needed. Transfer to a small serving bowl and place the bowl on a platter. Arrange an assortment of vegetables alongside it for serving.

**FOR THE DIP**

2 tablespoons unsalted butter
2 medium yellow onions, finely chopped
Kosher salt and freshly ground black pepper
1½ tablespoons balsamic vinegar
1 teaspoon packed light brown sugar
4 ounces cream cheese, cut into chunks, at room temperature
1 cup sour cream
⅓ cup mayonnaise
2 teaspoons Worcestershire sauce
¼ teaspoon onion powder
¼ teaspoon garlic powder

**FOR SERVING**

Cucumber slices or spears (Persian cucumbers are nice)
Zucchini spears
Baby rainbow carrots or carrot spears
Radishes, trimmed and quartered (if large)
Small celery stalks (with some baby leaves)
Sugar snap peas

OUR FIVE MARYS JERKY IS one of the most popular items we sell. It's the perfect snack for outdoor adventures, road trips, or a picnic lunch. Sometimes we make it at home because it's a fun and easy weekend project if we're hanging around the house for a few hours doing other chores or stuck inside in inclement weather while Brian is out tending to the animals. At the Farm Store, we offer several kinds of jerky, including a traditional smoked whiskey-maple beef; beef snack strips (a.k.a. "meat candy," which are a thicker, juicier variation glazed in sticky-sweet deliciousness); and three flavors of meat snack sticks: teriyaki, salami, and pepperoni. Our girls love them in their school lunches or their backpacks for a hiking adventure on the mountain.

# TERIYAKI BEEF JERKY

*Makes about ½ pound jerky*

Wrap the steak in plastic wrap and place it in the freezer for about 1 hour (this makes it a little easier to slice thinly). Unwrap the steak and, using a very sharp knife, cut it against the grain into ⅛- to ¼-inch-thick slices. Transfer to a baking dish.

In a small bowl, whisk together the remaining ingredients, then pour the mixture over the steak. Cover the dish and marinate the steak in the refrigerator for at least 6 hours or up to overnight.

After the steak has marinated, line a baking sheet with aluminum foil. Remove the steak strips from the marinade, letting the excess drip off. Transfer to paper towels and use more paper towels to blot dry (the drier the steak, the sooner the jerky will be ready).

Spray a cooling rack with nonstick spray, and place it on the lined baking sheet. Arrange the steak strips on the cooling rack, laying them flat and making sure there is space between each strip.

Turn on the oven to 175 degrees F. Bake until the jerky is dried but still pliable, about 2½ to 3 hours. Be sure to check it often toward the end so the jerky doesn't overcook and become dry and tough. The jerky will keep refrigerated in an airtight container for 3 weeks.

1 to 1½ pounds sirloin or round steak, all fat trimmed
¼ cup Worcestershire sauce
¼ cup soy sauce
1 tablespoon packed light brown sugar (optional)
1 teaspoon freshly ground black pepper
½ to 1 teaspoon red pepper flakes
½ teaspoon garlic powder
½ teaspoon onion powder
½ teaspoon ground ginger

IN THE SUMMER MONTHS, we spend most nights in the open-air kitchen at Camp, where we have a long wooden table that seats lots of family or other visitors. When the grill is fired up and everyone is hungry but dinner is still a little ways away, I make these simple-but-hearty toasts. They disappear quickly! For a party, double the recipe and cut the toasts into quarters to make them easy to pick up while mingling. This is a perfect way to take advantage of all those late-season summer tomatoes from the garden.

# GRILLED CAPRESE TOASTS

*Makes 6 servings*

Prepare a grill for direct cooking over medium heat (about 400 degrees F). Brush the bread slices lightly on both sides with olive oil. Grill the bread, turning once, until toasted and grill-marked, about 3 minutes total. Watch carefully so it doesn't burn.

Spread the pesto thickly over each toast, about 1 tablespoon per slice. Top each toast with 2 or 3 slices of mozzarella, then 2 slices of tomato. Season with salt and pepper. In a bowl, toss the arugula with a drizzle of olive oil, the balsamic, and a pinch of salt. Top each toast with a pile of the dressed arugula. (If you don't use arugula, simply drizzle the toasts with balsamic.) Top with some basil and serve at once.

6 large ¾-inch-thick slices crusty country bread
Extra-virgin olive oil
⅓ cup fresh or store-bought basil pesto
About 9 ounces fresh mozzarella, cut into ¼-inch-thick slices
2 or 3 ripe tomatoes, preferably heirloom, cut into ¼-inch-thick slices
Kosher salt and freshly ground black pepper
1½ cups baby arugula (optional)
½ teaspoon balsamic vinegar
¼ cup roughly torn fresh basil leaves

SHAVED STEAK CARPACCIO MIGHT sound fancy, but it's really just a protein-packed salad that's relatively easy to put together. It's great served with sweet onions, toasted nuts, and peppery arugula like we do at the Burgerhouse. Making it yourself is simpler than you think and sure to earn rave reviews. By freezing the steak for a short amount of time, it becomes easy to slice paper-thin for that classic carpaccio texture. This is a good way to use beef tenderloin "tips," which are more difficult to cook evenly when roasting a whole tenderloin (which we love to do for holidays; see page 124). The salad is also delicious wrapped up between two pieces of bread or toast for a carpaccio sandwich.

# SHAVED STEAK CARPACCIO <u>WITH</u> PICKLED ONIONS, PINE NUTS, AND ARUGULA

*Makes 6 servings*

To make the pickled onions, place the onion in a small heatproof bowl and add boiling water to cover. Let soak for about 2 minutes, then drain in a colander. In a small saucepan over medium heat, bring the vinegar, garlic, sugar, and a pinch of salt to a boil, whisking until the sugar dissolves. Stir in the onion, then remove from the heat. Let cool to room temperature, then transfer to an airtight container and refrigerate until chilled, at least 30 minutes. (You can make and store the onions in the refrigerator for up to 2 weeks ahead.)

Wrap the tenderloin in plastic wrap and place it in the freezer for about 1 hour (this makes it a little easier to slice thinly). While the meat is chilling, in a small, dry skillet over medium-low heat, toast the pine nuts, shaking the pan occasionally, until lightly toasted, about 3 minutes. Remove from the heat and let cool.

Unwrap the tenderloin and, using a very sharp knife, cut it against the grain into ⅛-inch-thick slices. Lay out sheets of plastic wrap and place each slice onto the plastic. Top with another piece of plastic and gently pound the meat with a meat mallet until paper-thin. Transfer to a baking sheet and keep refrigerated as you pound each piece of meat. Repeat until all of the meat is sliced and pounded.

Drain the pickled onions and discard the garlic. Divide the meat evenly among 6 chilled plates (you should have 2 to 3 ounces per person). Season with salt and drizzle with olive oil. Top with the pickled onions, arugula, and pine nuts, dividing them evenly among the plates. Serve at once, with the crackers alongside.

**FOR THE PICKLED ONIONS**
½ small red onion, thinly sliced
¼ cup unseasoned rice vinegar or white vinegar
1 clove garlic, smashed
½ teaspoon sugar
Kosher salt and freshly ground black pepper

**FOR THE SALAD**
¾ to 1 pound beef tenderloin, preferably from the tip end of the roast
2 to 3 tablespoons pine nuts
About 4 handfuls baby arugula or mixed greens
Kosher salt
Extra-virgin olive oil
Buttery or flatbread crackers, for serving

WHEN I GET ASKED IF THERE is anything I miss about living in the Bay Area, my answer is usually "just the sushi and great Asian food!" So when I'm craving Thai food or flavors, I love to make these lettuce cups. The bright, balanced notes in this dish are terrific with pork but also work with ground beef. Using lettuce cups makes a great starter or light lunch, but you can serve the spiced meat over a bowl of steamed rice or noodles for a heartier meal. Brian always has the sriracha close at hand no matter which way it's served!

# SESAME-LIME PORK LETTUCE CUPS

*Makes about 16 lettuce cups*

Halve the head of lettuce and remove the core. Separate the inner leaves so you have 16 to 20 that are about 5 inches in diameter (larger leaves could be cut in half). Transfer to a plate and put in the refrigerator until ready to serve.

Heat a heavy skillet (preferably cast-iron) over medium-high heat, and cook the pork, garlic, and ginger, stirring occasionally, until the pork is browned, about 5 minutes. Pour off and discard any excess fat if you like.

Reduce the heat to medium, then stir in the onion, lime juice, fish sauce, brown sugar, sesame oil, and red pepper flakes. Cook, stirring, until the mixture becomes fragrant, about 1 minute, then remove from the heat. Stir in about three-quarters of the cilantro and season with salt.

Transfer the pork mixture to a shallow serving bowl and garnish with the remaining cilantro and the peanuts. Serve with the lettuce leaves alongside. To assemble, spoon a few tablespoons of the pork mixture into a lettuce leaf, then wrap and eat.

1 head butter lettuce or iceberg lettuce
1 pound ground pork
3 cloves garlic, minced
2 teaspoons grated fresh ginger
¼ red onion, very thinly sliced (about ½ cup)
2 tablespoons freshly squeezed lime juice
1½ tablespoons fish sauce
1 tablespoon packed light brown sugar
2 teaspoons toasted sesame oil
¼ teaspoon red pepper flakes
½ cup chopped fresh cilantro leaves
Kosher salt
¼ cup chopped roasted peanuts or cashews

NACHOS ARE A GREAT APPETIZER for a gathering and sometimes all you need for a family-style grazing dinner. Topped with melty queso, grilled marinated skirt steak, and plenty of jalapeños, they are the perfect crowd-pleaser. This recipe is a jumping-off point, so add whatever you love to your nachos. They are equally amazing with pulled pork (page 141) instead of the carne asada, or put the carne asada on tacos. If you're just craving some yummy queso and don't want to go the extra mile, simply make that (it's easily doubled) and serve with a heaping pile of tortilla chips and guacamole. You can double or even triple this recipe if you have a lot of hungry folks to feed.

# LOADED CARNE ASADA NACHOS

*Makes 6 servings*

To make the carne asada, in a small bowl, whisk together all of the ingredients except the steak. Put the steak in a baking dish and pour the marinade over it, turning to coat. Cover and refrigerate for at least 30 minutes or up to overnight.

To make the queso, in a medium saucepan over medium heat, melt the butter. Add the jalapeño and cook, stirring, for 1 minute. Sprinkle the flour over it and whisk until smooth, letting it bubble for 1 minute. Slowly add the milk, whisking constantly, until the mixture is smooth and starts to bubble, about 2 minutes. Add the cheddar in small handfuls, stirring gently until each addition is melted. Add the American cheese a little at a time, stirring until the mixture is smooth. Remove from the heat, cover, and set aside.

Preheat the oven to 375 degrees F. Line a large rimmed baking sheet with aluminum foil.

To cook the steak, prepare a grill for direct cooking over medium-high heat (400 to 450 degrees F), or heat a cast-iron stovetop grill pan. Remove the steak from the marinade and shake off the excess. Place the steak on the grill and cook, turning once, until nicely browned, 5 to 7 minutes for medium-rare (depending on how thick the steak is). Transfer the steak to a cutting board and let it rest for 5 minutes.

To assemble the nachos, cut the steak across the grain into thin strips, then chop into bite-size pieces. Spread the tortilla chips on the baking sheet, top with the steak, and bake for about 8 minutes, or until the chips start to warm. Meanwhile, rewarm the queso over low heat, stirring occasionally, until hot. Drizzle the nachos with the cheese sauce. Top with the salsa, jalapeños, onion, and cilantro. Serve at once.

**FOR THE CARNE ASADA**
Juice of 1 medium lime (about 2 tablespoons)
1 tablespoon extra-virgin olive oil
1 teaspoon chili powder
½ teaspoon ground cumin
½ teaspoon dried oregano
½ teaspoon kosher salt
¼ teaspoon freshly ground black pepper
¼ teaspoon garlic powder
1 pound skirt or flap steak, cut into 4-inch portions

**FOR THE QUESO**
2 tablespoons unsalted butter
1 small jalapeño, seeded and minced (optional)
2 tablespoons all-purpose flour
1 cup whole milk
1½ cups (4 ounces) shredded sharp cheddar cheese
1½ cups (4 ounces) American cheese, chopped

**FOR THE NACHOS**
12 to 14 ounces tortilla chips
About ¾ cup salsa, plus more for serving
About ½ cup pickled jalapeño slices, drained
About 3 tablespoons finely chopped red or white onion
⅓ cup chopped fresh cilantro leaves

# FREE-RANGE KIDS

Trading our suburban life for rural living had some surprising results. We switched out sneakers for muddy boots (or no shoes at all!), bouncy-house birthday parties for fence fixing, and walks to the park for ATV rides on the mountain. We knew it would be a much different lifestyle, but one thing that we couldn't have predicted was the effect it would have on our children. By necessity, life works differently on a ranch. Children have to be more independent, and more is expected of them.

Very soon after we moved, we started seeing big changes in our kids, especially in their self-sufficiency and capabilities and also in the way we parented. We could no longer cater to their every request like we did in the past; we didn't have the time, so we naturally took a step back and started parenting less.

It didn't happen overnight. Some things they just started doing on their own because Brian or I were occupied taking care of a sick animal or delivering piglets. But even when I was there, if they asked me to do something, I first asked myself whether they could do it themselves—make a sandwich, start a load of laundry, hang a shelf in their room—and, if it seemed reasonable, I put it right back on them, giving them the tools and a lesson on how to do it properly, or handing them a power drill. And they did it! Each time, I saw a sense of satisfaction and accomplishment that I hadn't seen before. When I expected more from them, they rose to the challenge and they were proud of themselves.

These days I'll come back to the house and find Francie baking or taking it upon herself to make dinner. At age twelve, she can operate the tractor, and Maisie, who is eleven, can herd cattle by herself with the ATV. She often helps her younger sisters around the house if I'm out with Brian working on ranch dilemmas that inevitably creep up. Nine-year-old Janie proudly learned to safely use a pocketknife so she can cut open bales of hay and feed the cows off the back of our old diesel truck, and even seven-year-old Tess can steer the truck—honking at the cows to get out of the way—so that they can be fed. The smile on her face when she climbs out of the cab is priceless.

I appreciate the resourcefulness and independence they've gained over the years, especially because they are all very important contributors to our ranching operation these days!

Beef

**B**EEF IS THE CORE OF our business, and Brian and I take great pride in producing a super-premium product for our customers. It takes a lot of resources to make high-quality beef. It requires pairing the right genetic lines with the right nutrition in the right environment. Unwavering daily care, attention, and adjustments on these fronts are our top priorities.

When we moved to the ranch, we knew that Black Angus was the breed of cattle we wanted to raise because they consistently produce exceptional meat with fantastic flavor and tenderness. High-quality Black Angus programs are known for their excellent heredity in producing, among other things, hardy and healthy calves and well-marbled meat. When we started our herd, we sourced from the best breeding programs on the West Coast to find these qualities in our cattle.

Cattle in our meat program live on pasture and eat grasses and alfalfa their entire lives, and they are finished on alfalfa, grass hay, and barley. We feed a steam-flaked, non-GMO barley, which contributes to flavor and marbling, and the cattle love it. We never use any growth hormones nor antibiotics, unless it's necessary to save an animal's life. If we do, that animal is not included in our meat program. We want our customers to know that all the meat we sell is 100-percent antibiotic-free.

Brian and I believe strongly in taking the extra time and care to raise healthy, all-natural cattle. Our bestselling cuts include the over-the-top tomahawk steak, a two-inch-thick rib eye with a long bone; our porterhouse steak with a well-marbled New York strip on one side and tender fillet just over the bone; and our ground beef.

We dry-age the whole carcass at harvest, so even the ground beef is dry-aged, and it makes a big difference in the taste and quality (for more on dry-aging, see page 99). For me, there's nothing better than a dry-aged New York strip steak seared in a hot cast-iron pan with lots of butter and a little sage. I serve it hot and thinly sliced, still on the cutting board, making the rounds to eager guests while I'm prepping the rest of dinner. Brian's go-to steak is a thick-cut rib eye grilled over oak wood on his favorite grill up at Camp. At the Burgerhouse, we offer steak strips on the menu, which are thin-cut sirloin with a side of crispy fries; the girls order it almost every time we go, even as an after-school snack. I've even had customers ask whether a round steak was a filet mignon because it was so tender and flavorful!

**THIS BURGER IS FAR AND AWAY** our number one best seller at the Burgerhouse—there's something about a cheeseburger partnered with the sweet bacon marmalade. The accompaniment was actually Brian's inspiration—the saltiness of the bacon and sweetness of the marmalade bring out the beefy flavor of the meat—and it's an easy thing to make and will last for up to one week in an airtight container in the fridge. We like to make a big batch and always have it on hand at home too.

# FIVE MARYS CHEESEBURGER WITH BACON MARMALADE

*Makes 6 burgers*

To make the bacon marmalade, in a large heavy skillet over medium heat, cook the bacon until browned but not crisp, stirring often, 8 to 10 minutes. Using a slotted spoon, transfer the bacon to paper towels to drain. Pour off all but 3 tablespoons of the fat in the pan.

Add the onion to the skillet and cook, stirring often, until softened but not browned, about 5 minutes. Add the garlic and cook just until fragrant, about 30 seconds. Add the reserved bacon, the coffee, brown sugar, maple syrup, and vinegar. Bring to a gentle boil, then reduce the heat to low and simmer gently, stirring occasionally, until thickened, about 20 minutes.

Let the mixture cool, then pulse in a food processor until it is the consistency of a spread that holds together but is still a little chunky. Season to taste with salt and pepper. The marmalade can be made up to 1 week in advance and stored in an airtight container in the refrigerator.

To make the burgers, divide the beef into six equal portions and gently form into patties about 4 inches wide and ¾ inch thick with straight sides. Season the patties generously with salt and pepper. Cover loosely and let the beef sit at room temperature for about 20 minutes. Meanwhile, prepare a grill for direct cooking over high heat (450 to 500 degrees F).

Grill the patties with the lid closed, turning once, until cooked to the preferred doneness, about 7 minutes total for medium-rare. Lay a slice of cheddar on each patty, cover the grill, and cook just to soften the cheese, about 30 seconds. Transfer the patties to a serving board. Toast the buns cut side down on the grill, then transfer to the board.

To build the burgers, spread the buns with mayonnaise. Place lettuce on each bottom bun, then a patty, then a big spoonful of bacon marmalade. Top with red onion and tomato, and serve with pickles on the side.

**FOR THE BACON MARMALADE**
1 pound thick-cut smoked bacon, finely chopped
1 small yellow onion, finely chopped
2 cloves garlic, minced
½ cup brewed strong coffee
¼ cup packed light brown sugar
¼ cup maple syrup
2 tablespoons apple cider vinegar
Kosher salt and freshly ground pepper

**FOR THE BURGERS**
2 pounds ground beef, preferably chuck or sirloin
Kosher salt and freshly ground black pepper, or M5 Spice Rub (see page 127)
6 (1-ounce) slices sharp cheddar cheese
6 brioche burger buns, split
Mayonnaise
6 leaves lettuce
6 thin slices red onion (optional)
6 slices tomato (optional)
Sliced dill pickles or bread-and-butter pickles, for serving (optional)

BEEF

WE ALL CRAVE SOME GREENS with our steak at times, and this is my idea of the salad that offers the best of both worlds: lots of avocado, fresh veggies, earthy pistachios, creamy dressing, and tender slices of beef. This version of green goddess dressing includes avocado and plenty of fresh herbs, and you can put it on just about anything. Add any other veggies you like for an even heartier salad.

# STEAK SALAD WITH GRILLED VEGETABLES, PISTACHIOS, AND GREEN GODDESS DRESSING

*Makes 6 servings*

To make the dressing, put all the ingredients in a blender and blend until smooth. Set aside or transfer to an airtight container and refrigerate until ready to use, up to 3 days. You should have 1 heaping cup of dressing.

To make the salad, pat the steaks dry with paper towels, brush lightly with oil, and season generously with salt and pepper. Let sit at room temperature for 30 minutes.

Prepare a grill for direct cooking over high heat (450 to 500 degrees F). Brush the grates clean. Place the zucchini, bell pepper, and onion on a baking sheet. Brush the vegetables all over with oil and season lightly with salt.

Transfer the vegetables to the grate and grill with the lid closed, turning occasionally, until grilled-marked and crisp-tender, 3 to 6 minutes. Return them to the baking sheet as they finish cooking; the zucchini will take 3 to 4 minutes, the onion will take 5 minutes, and the pepper will take about 6 minutes. Set aside.

Grill the steaks with the lid closed until they are cooked to the preferred doneness, about 8 minutes total for medium-rare (125 to 130 degrees F). To make sure the steaks cook evenly, reposition them and flip once or twice during cooking. Transfer the steaks to a cutting board to rest for 10 minutes.

Roughly chop the zucchini, peppers, and onion and add to a mixing bowl along with the lettuce and ¼ cup of the dressing. Toss to coat evenly, then divide the salad among six plates or pile it onto a platter. Thinly slice the steak across the grain and arrange it over the salads. Top with the avocado, season with a little salt, and garnish with the pistachios. Serve at once, passing the remaining dressing along with lemon wedges on the side for squeezing over the salads.

**FOR THE DRESSING**
½ cup mayonnaise
¼ cup well-shaken buttermilk
¼ large ripe avocado
1 green onion (white and green parts), chopped
1 tablespoon chopped fresh tarragon or dill
1 tablespoon chopped fresh chives
1 tablespoon chopped fresh flat-leaf parsley
Juice of ½ large lemon (about 2 tablespoons)

**FOR THE SALAD**
2 pounds boneless steaks, such as top sirloin or rib eye, each about 1 inch thick and trimmed of excess fat
Extra-virgin olive oil
Kosher salt and freshly ground black pepper
2 small zucchini, cut lengthwise into ½-inch-thick slices
1 large red bell pepper, quartered
3 (½-inch-thick) slices red onion
5 to 7 ounces mixed baby lettuces, spinach, and/or watercress
¾ large ripe avocado, sliced
¼ cup salted roasted pistachios, for garnish
Lemon wedges, for serving

# GRASS FED AND GRAIN FINISHED

We firmly believe that grass feeding and grain finishing gives beef a fantastic flavor and results in the highest-quality beef. That means starting with cattle that come from exceptional genetics—for example, animals that have great marbling. But it doesn't end there: the cattle have to be raised in the best possible conditions and given extra care. Our cattle live a grass-fed lifestyle, out on the pasture every day, grazing on homegrown alfalfa and timothy grasses. For their optimal health, we have carefully formulated mineral salts based on our soil and their diet. We grain finish with steam-flaked barley. Our cattle love it, and it's naturally GMO-free. We started ranching to be able to provide this super-premium product to feed our family and customers, and we are proud to continue to do just that.

WHEN WE HAVE A PHYSICALLY demanding job to do like branding, it's all hands on deck. After hours of hard work, everyone is ready for a hearty afternoon lunch, and this is an ideal recipe for such occasions. You can leave out the beans if you prefer, or if you love them, add even more. Serve it as is, or put out a bunch of different toppings for everyone to create their own favorite chili bowl. And, of course, don't forget to make cornbread, its perfect companion, to serve alongside.

# COWBOY CHILI

*Makes 6 to 8 servings*

In a large heavy pot or Dutch oven over medium heat, warm the oil. Add the onion, bell peppers, and a pinch of salt and cook, stirring, until the vegetables soften and start to brown, about 8 minutes. Increase the heat to medium-high, add the beef, and cook, stirring, until it is no longer pink, about 5 minutes.

Add all of the spices plus 1 teaspoon salt and ½ teaspoon black pepper and stir until well combined and fragrant. Add the beans, tomatoes and their juices, and water. Bring to a boil, then reduce the heat to low, and cook, stirring occasionally, until the chili is thick and rich, about 1 hour. (If it gets too thick, add a little more water.) Taste and season with more salt and pepper if you like.

Serve bowlfuls of chili topped with cheese, sour cream, and/or onions and the cornbread on the side.

2 tablespoons extra-virgin olive oil
1 medium yellow onion, finely chopped
1 medium red bell pepper, diced
1 small green bell pepper, diced
Kosher salt and freshly ground black pepper
2 pounds ground beef, preferably chuck or sirloin
¼ cup chili powder
1 teaspoon ground cumin
1 teaspoon ground coriander
1 teaspoon smoked paprika
½ teaspoon garlic powder
½ teaspoon cayenne
2 (15-ounce) cans pinto beans, rinsed and drained
1 (28-ounce) can crushed tomatoes
1 (15-ounce) can diced tomatoes
1 cup water

**FOR SERVING**
1 cup shredded Monterey Jack or cheddar cheese
1 cup sour cream
½ cup chopped green or red onions
Skillet Cornbread with Honey Butter (page 211)

BEEF

CHILI PLUS MAC AND CHEESE is a match made in heaven. If you manage to have leftover chili (it doesn't happen often at our house!), this is a great solution to create a second satisfying meal that will disappear fast. My girls love it so much that sometimes I just make a double batch of chili so we are sure to have enough for this. Of course, this mac and cheese is a classic crowd-pleaser on its own. You can even stir some sautéed mushrooms, peas, or blanched broccoli or cauliflower florets into the mac and cheese before baking for a veggie-full variation.

# LEFTOVER CHILI MAC AND CHEESE

*Makes 6 servings*

Preheat the oven to 400 degrees F. Grease a 9-by-13-inch baking dish.

Bring a large saucepan filled halfway with salted water to a boil. Add the macaroni and cook just until al dente (it will continue to cook in the oven), about 4 minutes or according to package directions. Drain in a colander, rinse with cold water, and set aside.

In the same saucepan over medium-low heat, melt the butter. Sprinkle the flour over it and whisk until smooth. Slowly add the milk, whisking constantly until smooth. Let simmer for about 2 minutes to thicken slightly. Slowly add the cheese, whisking until smooth. Season with salt and pepper. Add the macaroni and stir until well combined.

Spread the chili in an even layer in the baking dish. Scrape the mac and cheese over the chili and spread into an even layer. Bake until bubbly and lightly browned around the edges, about 20 minutes. Let stand for 5 minutes before serving.

1 pound elbow macaroni
   or penne
5 tablespoons unsalted butter
⅓ cup all-purpose flour
3¼ cups whole milk
8 ounces white cheddar,
   shredded (about 3 cups)
Kosher salt and freshly ground
   black pepper
4 cups leftover Cowboy Chili
   (page 87), warmed

BEEF

TAMALE PIE IS A MARRIAGE of chili-laced beef beneath a tender cornbread crust. Pops of sweet corn and flavorful enchilada sauce give the beef plenty of rich flavor, and it all comes together in one cast-iron pan, making for easy serving and cleanup. Cast iron gives this dish a great caramelized crust because it retains heat so well. If you like, add a can of rinsed and drained black beans to the filling, or stir a big handful of shredded cheddar or Jack cheese into the cornbread batter. Serve it with a big dollop of sour cream and of course avocado, hot sauce, and plenty of sliced jalapeños!

# CAST-IRON TAMALE PIE

*Makes 6 servings*

Preheat the oven to 425 degrees F.

To make the filling, in a 10-inch cast-iron pan over medium heat, warm the oil. Add the onion and cook, stirring, until softened and lightly golden, about 6 minutes. Add the beef and cook, stirring and chopping it up, until no longer pink, about 5 minutes. Drain off excess fat. Add the chili powder and cumin and stir to combine, then stir in the enchilada sauce. Reduce the heat to low and simmer until slightly thickened, 12 to 15 minutes.

Meanwhile, to make the cornbread topping, in a large bowl, whisk together the cornmeal, flour, sugar, baking powder, and salt. In another bowl, whisk together the milk, egg, and oil. Add the wet mixture to the dry mixture and stir to combine.

Stir the corn and cilantro into the meat filling. Pour the cornbread batter over the top in an even layer.

Bake the pie until bubbly and the cornbread is cooked through, about 18 minutes. Serve with a big dollop of sour cream and some hot sauce.

**FOR THE FILLING**
1 tablespoon canola oil
½ medium yellow onion, finely chopped
1½ pounds ground beef, preferably chuck or sirloin
2 teaspoons chili powder
1 teaspoon ground cumin
1 (15-ounce) can mild or spicy red enchilada sauce
½ cup frozen corn kernels
¼ cup chopped fresh cilantro leaves

**FOR THE CORNBREAD TOPPING**
½ cup fine cornmeal
½ cup all-purpose flour
2 tablespoons sugar
1½ teaspoons baking powder
½ teaspoon kosher salt
½ cup whole milk
1 large egg
2 tablespoons canola oil

**FOR SERVING (OPTIONAL)**
Sour cream
Hot sauce
Sliced green onions
Fresh cilantro leaves

# CARING FOR CAST IRON

At the ranch, we have just about every size and shape of cast-iron pan you can imagine, from the smallest individual ones for baking little cobblers to massive skillets that will create a feast for a crowd. Cast iron is a great material because it's heavy duty, it can go from oven to stovetop to grill to open fire, it retains heat once it's warmed through, and it will create a crust you simply can't get from many pans. If it's well seasoned, you can even fry an egg in it without sticking! One of my favorite things to do is search flea markets or antique fairs for a rusty old skillet everyone else passes by.

Restoring a pan to its former glory is a challenge, but there's nothing better than seeing a trustworthy piece of cookware come back to life. I've found that the best way to upgrade a crusty pan is to throw it into a roaring fire and burn all the grime away, or get it nice and hot in the oven. While the pan is hot—be sure to wear a heatproof glove!—use a knife or fork to scrape any gunk off until you are down to the bare iron (chain-mail scrubbers are great for this). Let it cool down, then use a clean rag to wipe the pan with a high-smoke-point oil, such as vegetable oil or lard (avoid using olive oil). Heat the pan either over medium heat on the stovetop or upside down in a 375-degree oven (with a pan beneath to catch the drips) for 1 hour. Remove from the heat and let cool, then season the pan again with the same oil and reheat in the same manner once more. If you can, repeat this process a third time. The more times you do it, the better seasoned the pan will be.

When I'm cooking with cast iron, I always make sure the pan is hot before I add any ingredients. I can cook scrambled eggs in a searing-hot pan and they won't stick, but adding them to a cold pan is sure to leave you scrubbing (and cursing) afterward! If any food does stick during cooking, leave the heat on and add some water to the empty pan. Once it starts simmering, use a silicone spatula to gently scrape the bottom and loosen it up. For stubborn gunk, throw in a generous handful of coarse salt and warm the pan over low heat. Use a thick rag or chain-mail scrubber to work the salt in like an abrasive; this not only cleans the pan, it adds a little salt to its seasoning. Rinse it under hot water but avoid using soap, then dry it thoroughly with a clean rag. *Never air-dry cast iron or it will rust.* Whenever possible, add a little more oil to the inside of the pan before putting it away, and it will be ready for the next use.

I LOVE THIS SOUP! I have so many memories of simmering a big pot of it on the stove-top in our early days on the ranch, waiting for Brian when he finally found a minute to stop for lunch. He was always so thrilled to come in and find a steaming bowl of this hearty, flavorful soup on the table. The potatoes give it a comfort-food feel, plus it's easy to make any time of year and an excellent way to use extra ground beef. I often make a big batch just to have it in the fridge. It's a meal that keeps us going until well after dark once we've finished our chores. This soup was originally inspired by Ree Drummond's delicious recipe (she adds canned corn), but we've put our own spin on it and you can too—it's really easy to adapt with your favorites!

# HAMBURGER SOUP

*Makes 6 servings*

In a large heavy pot or Dutch oven over medium heat, warm the oil. Add the onion, celery, and a big pinch of salt and cook, stirring, until the onion is softened, about 5 minutes. Add the garlic and cook until fragrant, about 1 minute. Add the beef and cook, stirring occasionally, until no longer pink, about 5 minutes. Drain the fat as needed, then return the pot to the heat. Add the diced tomatoes with juices and tomato paste, and stir until well combined. Stir in the stock, potatoes, carrots, bell pepper, kidney beans, 1 teaspoon salt, ½ teaspoon black pepper, and the cayenne.

Increase to medium-high heat to bring the soup to a boil, then reduce the heat to low, partially cover, and simmer until the potatoes are tender but not mushy, 30 to 45 minutes. Adjust the thickness of the soup with additional stock if needed. Taste and season with more salt, pepper, and cayenne if you like. Serve with crusty bread.

1 tablespoon extra-virgin olive oil
1 medium yellow onion, finely chopped
2 stalks celery, finely chopped
Kosher salt and freshly ground black pepper
3 cloves garlic, minced
2 pounds ground beef, preferably chuck or sirloin
1 (14.5-ounce) can diced tomatoes
¼ cup tomato paste
3 cups low-sodium beef stock, plus more if needed
1 pound small red potatoes, quartered
2 carrots, peeled, halved lengthwise, and cut into ½-inch-thick slices
1 large red bell pepper, diced
1 (14.5-ounce) can red kidney beans, rinsed and drained
¼ teaspoon cayenne
Crusty bread, for serving

SHOWING OFF THE EFFORT WE put into producing exceptional beef by serving a perfectly grilled steak is a highlight for Brian and me. When we have guests at the ranch, we pull out the best steaks from our family pile, and it's a treat for everyone. The taste of quality beef infused with wood smoke and charred by flames is always memorable. Although a great steak doesn't need much else, this umami-rich sauce really elevates it. Porterhouse is one of our favorite cuts because you get both the strip and the tenderloin, but this recipe works well with T-bones, rib eyes, or even the tomahawk steak—just be aware that cook times vary slightly.

# WOOD-FIRED PORTERHOUSE STEAK WITH MUSHROOM-SHALLOT SAUCE

*Makes 6 servings*

Pat the steaks dry with a paper towel, then rub some oil into both sides of the meat. Season evenly with the rub (or plenty of salt and pepper). Set aside at room temperature while you make the sauce and fire up the grill.

To make the sauce, in a large skillet over medium heat, melt the butter. Add the shallot and cook until softened, about 2 minutes. Add the mushrooms and a pinch of salt and cook until they release liquid, about 5 minutes. Add the garlic and rosemary and cook until fragrant, about 2 minutes. Stir in the balsamic, soy sauce, and Worcestershire; increase the heat to medium-high and simmer until the sauce starts to reduce slightly but is still saucy and the mushrooms are tender, 3 to 4 minutes. Season with salt and pepper. Remove from the heat and cover to keep warm.

Set up a wood fire for grilling using hardwood, or prepare a charcoal or gas grill for direct and indirect cooking over medium-high heat (400 to 450 degrees F). Brush the grates clean.

Grill the steaks over direct heat with the lid closed until cooked to the preferred doneness, 10 to 14 minutes for medium-rare (125 to 130 degrees F). To ensure the steaks cook evenly, reposition and flip them once or twice during cooking. If the steaks need to cook longer, move them to the indirect heat.

Let the steaks rest for 10 minutes while you rewarm the sauce. To serve, first cut the meat away from the bone, then cut across the grain into ⅓-inch-thick slices. Serve with plenty of sauce spooned over the top.

**FOR THE STEAKS**
3 (1-pound, 1¼- to 1½-inch-thick) well-marbled Porterhouse steaks
Extra-virgin olive oil
M5 Spice Rub (see page 127), or kosher salt and freshly ground black pepper

**FOR THE SAUCE**
6 tablespoons unsalted butter
2 medium shallots, minced
1½ pounds cremini or button mushrooms, sliced
Kosher salt and freshly ground black pepper
2 cloves garlic, minced
1 teaspoon minced fresh rosemary leaves
¼ cup balsamic vinegar
2 tablespoons low-sodium soy sauce
2 tablespoons Worcestershire sauce

# DRY-AGING:
# A CRAFT TRADITION

Pork or lamb can be eaten soon after harvesting, but that is not the case with beef. Beef benefits from aging to promote tenderness and enhance flavor. Shortly after slaughter, most beef sold in the United States is split into large pieces (or "primals"), vacuum-sealed, and boxed up for transport, where it wet-ages in the packaging so as not to lose as much volume during transit to grocery stores, meat distributors, and similar vendors. Upon arrival, it is ultimately portioned into steaks, roasts, and other cuts for the consumer. Ground beef and trim is often packaged and shipped without the benefit of any aging at all.

In contrast, dry-aging beef involves hanging it in a humidity-controlled room with ample air flow at just-above-freezing temperatures for at least fourteen days, and sometimes longer. The dry-aging process requires more effort, time, expertise, and expense, but it imparts a unique flavor and delicate consistency to the meat.

Dry-aging is a craft tradition that used to be the norm, but it is slowly being phased out in favor of expediency and efficiency. Brian and I firmly believe that dry-aging creates the best possible beef with that amazing "steak house" taste and tenderness every time. We don't cut a single steak or grind any meat until the entire carcass is dry-aged for twenty-one to twenty-eight days after harvest. Purely grass-fed beef doesn't always benefit from dry-aging as it is often too lean, but because we finish our cattle on barley, which results in great natural marbling, dry-aging is an essential part of what makes our beef unforgettable.

**IF YOU KNOW ME ENOUGH** to know how much I love jalapeños, you also know I love hot sauce equally well. And there is really nothing like homemade hot sauce. I grow a ridiculous number of chili peppers in my vegetable garden (we have a short growing season in the mountains and it can freeze any day of the year, but peppers are hearty enough to do really well here), so I can make gallons of green and red chili hot sauce to last me through the winter. This salsa, which is amazing on just about anything, can be as kicky as you want it to be—the spicier the better is just the way I like it. Adjust the heat by adding more or less peppers; deseeding them will also bring the heat level down a bit since that's where most of the spiciness resides.

# FLANK STEAK TACOS WITH ROASTED TOMATILLO SALSA

*Makes 6 servings*

To marinate the steak, in a small bowl, whisk together the oil, cumin, oregano, salt, and pepper. Put the steak in a baking dish and pour the marinade over it, turning to coat. Cover and refrigerate for at least 30 minutes or up to 10 hours.

To make the salsa, preheat the oven to 500 degrees F and line a large rimmed baking sheet with aluminum foil or parchment paper. Place the tomatillos, onion, chilies, and garlic on the baking sheet, drizzle with the oil, and toss to coat. Roast until the skins start to darken and the tomatillos soften, 15 to 20 minutes. Scrape the mixture into the bowl of a food processor, including any juices. Add the cilantro, lime juice, and a big pinch of salt and pulse to the desired consistency (add a little water if the salsa is too thick). Transfer to a bowl and season with additional salt if needed. Set aside to cool completely. (You should have 2½ cups salsa.) Leftover salsa will keep for a week in the refrigerator.

To cook the steak, prepare a charcoal or gas grill for direct cooking over medium-high heat (400 to 450 degrees F) or heat a stovetop grill pan over medium-high heat. Brush the grates clean. Grill the steak with the lid closed, only turning once halfway through, until cooked to the preferred doneness, 8 to 10 minutes total for medium-rare. Transfer the steak to a cutting board to rest for 5 minutes.

### FOR THE STEAK
1 tablespoon extra-virgin olive oil
1 teaspoon ground cumin
1 teaspoon dried oregano
1 teaspoon kosher salt
½ teaspoon freshly ground black pepper
1½ pounds flank steak

### FOR THE SALSA
1½ pounds fresh tomatillos, husked
1 small white onion, quartered and cut crosswise into thick slices
2 or 3 jalapeños or serranos (depending on how spicy you like it), trimmed
2 large cloves garlic, peeled
2 tablespoons extra-virgin olive oil
½ bunch fresh cilantro, thick stems removed and leaves chopped
Juice of 1 medium lime (2 tablespoons)
Kosher salt

To serve, cut the steak against the grain into ¼-inch-thick slices and serve from the cutting board. Set out the tortillas alongside bowls of the tomatillo salsa, cheese, onion, cilantro, avocado, and lime wedges, and invite diners to build their tacos as they like. Squeeze the lime wedges over the top and enjoy at once.

**FOR SERVING**

12 (6-inch) corn tortillas, warmed

About ¾ cup crumbled cotija cheese

⅓ cup finely chopped white onion

⅓ cup chopped fresh cilantro leaves

2 ripe avocados, sliced

2 limes, cut into wedges

FLAT IRON STEAK IS A really flavorful, well-marbled cut from the shoulder of the steer that is gaining in popularity. If a customer at the Burgerhouse requests flank or skirt steak and we are out (there are only two of these "rare" cuts on one steer), we usually suggest a flat iron, and they are always sure to order it again. The marinated steak is worth making on its own with whatever sides you like, but the fries are outstanding if you have the time. We leave the potatoes unpeeled for a more rustic presentation (that's the way we love 'em), but you could peel them instead. Just try to cut them all the same size so they cook evenly. The garlic butter is delicious on any cut of steak, or spread on thick slices of toasted bread.

# FLAT IRON STEAK WITH GARLIC BUTTER AND FRIES

*Makes 6 servings*

Place the steaks on a baking sheet or dish. In a small bowl, whisk together the oil, Worcestershire, paprika, oregano, salt, and a few grinds of pepper. Rub the mixture into both sides of the meat. Set aside at room temperature for up to 1 hour or refrigerate up to overnight.

To make the fries, cut the potatoes lengthwise into ⅜-inch-thick slabs, then stack the slabs and cut lengthwise into ⅜-inch-thick batons. Transfer to a large bowl and add enough cold water to cover, along with the vinegar and 2 tablespoons salt. Set aside at room temperature to soak for at least 1 hour, or refrigerate up to overnight.

Meanwhile, make the garlic butter. Preheat the oven to 375 degrees F. Place the garlic on a piece of aluminum foil, drizzle with a little olive oil, and sprinkle with a pinch of salt. Close up the foil into a sealed pouch and bake until the cloves are soft, about 35 minutes. Squeeze the garlic out of the skins (discard the skins) into a small bowl. Add the butter and, using the tines of a fork, smash the garlic and butter together until smooth. Stir in the parsley and season with salt. Transfer to a piece of waxed paper or parchment and roll into a log. Refrigerate until ready to serve, up to 4 days in advance.

Line two large rimmed baking sheets with paper towels. Drain and rinse the potatoes in a fine-mesh sieve, then spread them onto one of the prepared baking sheets. Use another paper towel to blot the potatoes as dry as possible.

## FOR THE STEAK
2 (1-pound) flat iron steaks
2 tablespoons extra-virgin olive oil
1 tablespoon Worcestershire sauce
1 teaspoon sweet paprika
1 teaspoon dried oregano
½ teaspoon kosher salt
Freshly ground black pepper

## FOR THE FRIES
2 pounds russet potatoes
2 tablespoons white vinegar
Kosher salt
Canola oil, for frying

## FOR THE GARLIC BUTTER
6 medium cloves garlic, unpeeled
Extra-virgin olive oil
Kosher salt
½ cup (1 stick) unsalted butter, at room temperature
1 tablespoon minced fresh flat-leaf parsley leaves

BEEF

➤——→

105

Pour enough oil into a wide, deep saucepan to come 1½ inches up the side of the pan. Place over medium-high heat, and warm the oil to 250 degrees F on a deep-fry thermometer. Fry the potatoes in three or four batches, using a heatproof slotted spoon to gently stir them so they don't stick, until cooked through but not browned, about 5 minutes. Adjust the heat as needed to maintain a steady temperature of 250 degrees F. Transfer them to the second baking sheet to drain as they finish cooking. Repeat with the remaining potatoes. Set aside to cool.

Prepare a charcoal or gas grill for direct cooking over medium-high heat (400 to 450 degrees F). Brush the grates clean. Grill the steaks with the lid closed, only turning once halfway through, until cooked to the preferred doneness, 8 to 10 minutes total for medium-rare. Transfer to a cutting board to rest for 5 to 10 minutes.

While the steaks rest, finish the fries. Preheat the oven to 200 degrees F. Set a wire rack in a rimmed baking sheet and place in the oven. Return the saucepan with oil to medium-high heat, and warm to 375 to 400 degrees F on a deep-fry thermometer. Fry half of the potatoes, using a slotted spoon to gently stir them, until crisp and golden brown, about 3 minutes. Drain on paper towels, sprinkle with salt, then transfer to the wire rack in the oven to keep warm while you cook the second batch. Transfer the second batch to the oven to keep warm while you cut the steaks.

To serve, cut the steaks against the grain into ⅓-inch-thick slices. Divide among six plates and top each serving with some garlic butter. Pile hot fries onto each plate and serve at once.

CHICKEN FRIED STEAK IS ONE of Brian's all-time favorite dishes. With a nod to its Southern roots, this version, made with high-quality steak, is over-the-top good. The type of steak you choose is nearly as important as its quality. If you use round steak, tenderize it first by pounding it with a studded meat mallet (or tenderizer tool) until it's as thin as possible. Cube steak is a version of top sirloin or top round that's been run through an electric tenderizer. This is such a brawny dish that it can seem unapproachable, but don't be afraid to try it at home.

# BRIAN'S CHICKEN FRIED STEAK <u>WITH</u> COUNTRY GRAVY

*Makes 6 servings*

To make the gravy, in a cast-iron skillet over medium heat, melt the butter. Whisk in the flour and cook, whisking constantly, until the roux turns a toasty golden brown, 2 to 3 minutes. Reduce the heat to low and slowly add the milk, whisking constantly, until well combined. Season with ½ teaspoon salt and ½ teaspoon pepper. Return the heat to medium and simmer, stirring constantly, until the gravy thickens to your liking, about 4 minutes. Season with more salt and pepper, if needed, and adjust the gravy thickness with a little milk if you like. Remove from the heat and cover to keep warm.

If using round steaks, place one steak on a cutting board and pound it with a studded meat mallet to an even thickness of ⅛ to ¼ inch. Repeat with all of the steaks. Season the steaks lightly on both sides with salt and place on a large rimmed baking sheet.

In a wide shallow dish or pie pan, whisk together the flour, 1½ teaspoons salt, onion powder, paprika, garlic powder, and pepper. In a second wide shallow dish, whisk together the eggs and milk. Working with one steak at a time, dredge the steak in the flour, pressing the mixture into the steak and then shaking off the excess. Dip the steak in the egg mixture, turning to coat and then letting the excess drip back into the dish. Finally, dredge in the flour a second time, pressing it into the steak and gently shaking off the excess. Return the steak to the baking sheet and repeat to coat all the steaks.

**FOR THE GRAVY**
¼ cup unsalted butter or bacon grease
¼ cup all-purpose flour
2½ cups whole milk, plus more if needed
Kosher salt and freshly ground black pepper

**FOR THE STEAK**
6 (4-ounce) round steaks or cube steaks
Kosher salt
2 cups all-purpose flour
1 teaspoon onion powder
1 teaspoon sweet paprika
½ teaspoon garlic powder
½ teaspoon freshly ground black pepper
2 large eggs
¼ cup whole milk
Canola or vegetable oil, for frying

➤——→

BEEF

Preheat the oven to 200 degrees F. Place a wire rack on a baking sheet and put it in the oven.

Fill a large heavy frying pan with enough oil to reach ¼ to ½ inch up the side. Place the pan over medium-high heat and warm the oil until hot but not smoking (350 degrees F on a deep-fry thermometer). In batches, fry the steaks, turning once, until the outsides are a crisp golden brown and the meat is just cooked through, about 4 minutes total. Transfer to the wire rack in the oven and repeat with the remaining steaks.

Rewarm the gravy over low heat, stirring, until hot. Serve the steaks at once with plenty of gravy over the top.

# SAUSAGE GRAVY VARIATION

To transform the country gravy into sausage gravy—perfect for topping fresh buttermilk biscuits (page 27)—simply sauté ¼ to ½ pound crumbled bulk breakfast sausage, homemade (page 32) or purchased, in the skillet until nicely browned. Add the flour and take it from there! You might need a tad more milk to get the gravy to the consistency you like.

SHEPHERD'S PIE, COTTAGE PIE, RANCHER'S PIE—they are all pretty similar in that they have a savory meat filling and lots of fluffy mashed potatoes crowning the top, and they are baked until bubbling and crispy brown. Traditionally shepherd's pie uses ground lamb, and it was a dish my Irish grandmother loved. Cottage pie is more of an English variation that uses beef. I call my version rancher's pie because I use whatever I have on hand, beef or lamb, but ground beef is my go-to. It's the perfect hearty dinner when temperatures start to drop in the evenings and you need something cozy and filling to warm you up. The mashed potatoes double as a fantastic side.

# RANCHER'S PIE

*Makes 6 servings*

To make the mashed potatoes, in a large saucepan filled with cold salted water, add the potatoes and bring to a boil over medium-high heat. Boil until tender when pierced with a paring knife, about 20 minutes. Drain in a colander, then return the potatoes to the saucepan. Add the milk and butter, and mash with a potato masher until smooth and creamy. Season with salt, then cover to keep warm.

Preheat the oven to 375 degrees F.

To make the filling, in a 12-inch ovenproof skillet with high sides over medium heat, melt 2 tablespoons of the butter. Add the carrots, celery, onion, and a sprinkle of salt and cook, stirring, until the vegetables become tender and start to brown, about 8 minutes. Add the garlic and cook until fragrant, about 30 seconds. Add the ground beef and cook until it is no longer pink, about 5 minutes. Drain off any excess fat. Stir in ¾ cup stock, the tomato paste, and Worcestershire. Season generously with salt and pepper. If the mixture is dry, add the remaining ¼ cup stock. Bring the mixture to a boil, then stir in the peas. Remove from the heat.

Top the beef mixture with dollops of warm mashed potatoes, then spread it into a thick, even layer. Draw the tines of a fork through the potatoes in a crosshatch to create ridges. Dot with the remaining 2 tablespoons butter.

Bake until the potatoes are golden brown on top and the filling is bubbling, about 30 minutes. Let stand 5 minutes before serving.

**FOR THE MASHED POTATOES**
2 pounds russet or Yukon Gold potatoes, peeled and cut into 1-inch pieces
½ cup whole milk, warmed
4 tablespoons unsalted butter
Kosher salt

**FOR THE FILLING**
4 tablespoons unsalted butter, divided
2 medium carrots, peeled and diced
2 stalks celery, diced
1 small yellow onion, finely chopped
Kosher salt and freshly ground black pepper
2 cloves garlic, minced
2 pounds ground beef, preferably chuck or sirloin, or ground lamb
¾ to 1 cup low-sodium beef stock
¼ cup tomato paste
3 tablespoons Worcestershire sauce
½ cup frozen petite peas

BEEF

WE OFTEN MAKE SHORT RIBS for our farm dinners and for retreats up at Camp because they feel decadent and special, but they couldn't be easier to make, and it's a cut that isn't overly expensive. The refreshing bite of the citrus gremolata—a mix of fresh herbs, garlic, and citrus zest—cuts through the richness of the meat and adds a pop of flavor. These ribs are excellent served over creamy polenta (page 200) or mashed potatoes. Be sure to choose English-style ribs, which are cut parallel to the bone, with one bone per piece (not flanken style, which are cut across the bone).

# BRAISED SHORT RIBS WITH CITRUS GREMOLATA

*Makes 6 servings*

Preheat the oven to 400 degrees F. Season the short ribs all over with salt and pepper.

In a large Dutch oven or heavy pot over high heat, warm the olive oil. Sear the short ribs on two meaty sides, in two batches to avoid overcrowding, turning once when the first side is richly golden brown, about 5 minutes total for each batch. Reduce the heat if the pot gets too hot. Transfer the short ribs to a plate. Pour off all but 2 tablespoons fat from the pot.

Return to medium-high heat and add the onion, carrot, celery, and a sprinkle of salt. Cook, stirring to scrape up any browned bits, until the vegetables soften, about 4 minutes. Add the garlic and cook until fragrant, about 1 minute. Add the wine and bring to a boil, cooking for about 30 seconds, then stir in the stock and return to a boil while stirring.

Return the short ribs with any juices to the pot, nestling them into the liquid as much as possible. Crush the herb sprigs slightly with your hands, then add them to the pot along with the bay leaf. Cover and transfer the pot to the oven. Cook for 30 minutes, then rearrange the ribs, making sure they are as submerged in the liquid as possible. Reduce the oven temperature to 300 degrees F, then cover the pot again and return to the oven. Cook until the ribs are very tender, about 2½ hours.

### FOR THE RIBS

About 5 pounds bone-in
  English-style short ribs
  (6 ribs)
Kosher salt and freshly ground
  black pepper
2 tablespoons extra-virgin
  olive oil
1 medium yellow onion, finely
  chopped
1 large carrot, diced
1 stalk celery, finely chopped
4 cloves garlic, minced
1 cup dry red wine
2 cups low-sodium chicken
  stock
4 sprigs fresh thyme
3 sprigs fresh marjoram
1 bay leaf
¼ cup unsalted butter

### FOR THE GREMOLATA

1 cup finely chopped fresh flat-
  leaf parsley leaves
¼ cup extra-virgin olive oil
Finely grated zest of 1 medium
  orange
Finely grated zest of 2 medium
  lemons
Juice of ½ medium lemon
  (about 2 tablespoons)
2 cloves garlic, minced
Pinch of kosher salt

Meanwhile, make the gremolata. In a small bowl, stir together the parsley, olive oil, citrus zests and juice, garlic, and salt.

When the ribs are ready, using a slotted spoon, gently transfer them to a warm serving platter. If you like, remove any large pieces of fat (or pull the meat from the bones in large pieces, discarding the fat). Strain the cooking juices through a fine-mesh sieve into a saucepan (you should have about 2 cups). Using a large metal spoon, skim off as much fat from the surface of the liquid as possible.

Bring the liquid to a gentle boil over medium heat and simmer until reduced slightly, about 3 minutes. Add the butter, stirring until fully melted and the sauce is smooth. Taste and adjust the seasoning with salt and pepper if needed. Pour the sauce over the ribs. Top with the gremolata, spooning it evenly over the ribs, then serve at once.

## SHORT-RIB LEFTOVERS

Rich and decadent short ribs are ideal for leftovers and can be transformed into all sorts of delicious meals. My family often devours the entire meal, but sometimes I manage to sneak a few more short ribs into the pot (or better yet, I double the recipe). That's when I love to get creative. Shredded short ribs are perfect on top of nachos or stuffed into tacos. You can mix the meat with your favorite marinara sauce and toss it with pasta or serve it over creamy polenta. Or stir your favorite barbecue sauce into the shredded meat and pile it on slider rolls for a party. You can also use chopped short ribs in place of the ground meat in tamale pie (page 90), for a really special dinner on a cold night. Short ribs can seem like a daunting cut since they need to be braised low and slow—but it's always worth the effort!

MY MOM HAS ALWAYS BEEN such a great cook, and when I was growing up, family dinnertime was always a priority. Most nights she had a hot meal ready when my dad got home from a long day at the office, and she always made it seem effortless while the four of us kids were running in and out of the house all day. This rich, hearty beef stew has always been one of her favorites. She typically cooks this on the stovetop, but to save time I will sometimes make it in my slow cooker. It's so easy to throw it together in the morning and let it slowly simmer throughout the day. Then when we come home tired and hungry from evening chores, it's hot and ready to eat! You can leave out the butter and flour if you like, but it makes the gravy nice and silky.

# JANNIE'S BEEF STEW

*Makes 6 to 8 servings*

In a large bowl, toss the beef cubes with the spice rub. In a large cast-iron pan over medium-high heat, warm the oil until very hot but not smoking. In batches, cook the meat in a single layer until richly browned on all sides, about 5 minutes. Transfer the meat to a 6- to 8-quart slow cooker.

Reduce the heat to medium and add the onion to the pan. Cook, stirring to scrape up all the meaty bits, until golden, about 5 minutes. Add the wine and vinegar and bring to a gentle boil to cook off some of the alcohol, scraping the pan again, for about 2 minutes. Add the stock and bring to a boil. Pour over the meat in the slow cooker.

Add the potatoes, carrots, parsnips, mushrooms, and bay leaves to the slow cooker, stir everything to combine, cover, and cook on low for 6 hours, or until the meat is very tender. Scoop out 2 cups of the cooking liquid and set aside.

In a small saucepan over medium-low heat, melt the butter. Whisk in the flour and cook for about 1 minute, then slowly add the reserved cooking liquid, whisking constantly. Stir in the Worcestershire, and season with salt and plenty of pepper. Stir the mixture into the stew. Taste and adjust the seasoning with more salt, pepper, and Worcestershire as needed. Continue to cook on low for 30 minutes longer to warm through.

Serve steaming bowlfuls garnished with parsley and pass the bread alongside.

4 pounds beef chuck or sirloin roast, trimmed of excess fat and cut into 1-inch cubes
1 tablespoon M5 Spice Rub (see page 127)
3 tablespoons canola oil
1 large yellow onion, finely chopped
1 cup dry red wine
2 tablespoons red wine vinegar
3 cups low-sodium beef stock
1½ pounds Yukon Gold or russet potatoes, peeled and cut into 1-inch chunks
1 pound carrots, peeled and cut into 1-inch chunks
¾ pound parsnips, peeled and cut into 1-inch chunks
½ pound button or cremini mushrooms, halved or quartered if large
2 bay leaves
2 tablespoons unsalted butter
¼ cup all-purpose flour
3 tablespoons Worcestershire sauce
Kosher salt and freshly ground black pepper
¼ cup chopped fresh flat-leaf parsley leaves, for garnish
Crusty bread, for serving

BRISKET IS A BOUNTIFUL CUT, so it's an ideal choice when you have many people to feed. It's amazing when barbecued on a smoker, but I think it's equally delicious braised in a heavy enameled cast-iron pot in the oven (or in my slow cooker when I'm going to be away all day). Brisket is a colossal piece of beef that is unique to cattle; it appears to hang under the neck but is actually part of the chest muscle. Because it is a muscle that gets used often, it requires a "low and slow" cooking approach. Brisket has two parts: the flat and the point. Left whole, it's called a "packer brisket" and can be upwards of ten pounds! The flat is slightly leaner and yields more meat (perfect for braising), whereas the point is fattier and especially delicious when smoked. This recipe is terrific served with potatoes and other veggies, but it can also be piled on buns and topped with Ranch-Barbecue Sauce (page 147) or used for tacos, burritos, or nachos with plenty of hot sauce.

# BEER-BRAISED BRISKET

*Makes 6 to 8 servings*

Preheat the oven to 325 degrees F. Pat the brisket dry, drizzle it all over with olive oil, then season evenly with the spice rub.

In a large Dutch oven or heavy pot over medium-high heat, warm 2 tablespoons olive oil. Add the brisket and sear, turning once, until two sides are deeply golden, about 10 minutes total. (If the brisket is too large for the pot, cut it in half and sear each piece separately.) Transfer the brisket to a plate. Pour off the fat and scrape out any burnt bits from the pot.

Return the pot to medium-high heat. Add 1 tablespoon olive oil to the pot, then add the onion, carrots, celery, and garlic and cook, stirring, until the vegetables start to brown, about 5 minutes. Stir in the tomatoes with juices and the beer. Return the brisket, fat side up, and any juices to the pot, tucking it into the liquid so it is mostly submerged. Cover tightly and transfer to the oven. Cook until the brisket is very tender, 3 to 3½ hours.

Transfer the brisket to a cutting board and let rest for 15 minutes. Meanwhile, strain the liquid through a sieve into a small saucepan, discarding the vegetables. Use a large metal spoon to skim off as much fat from the top as possible. Bring to a boil over high heat and cook until the sauce is reduced slightly, about 5 minutes. Season with salt and pepper.

Carve the brisket crosswise into ½-inch-thick slices or pull it into pieces. Transfer to a serving platter, drizzle with the sauce, and garnish with the parsley.

4 pounds flat-cut brisket
Extra-virgin olive oil
1 tablespoon M5 Spice Rub (see page 127)
1 medium yellow onion, roughly chopped
2 large carrots, roughly chopped
2 stalks celery, roughly chopped
6 cloves garlic, smashed
1 (15-ounce) can diced tomatoes
1 (12-ounce) bottle dark beer, such as Negra Modelo
Kosher salt and freshly ground black pepper
¼ cup fresh flat-leaf parsley leaves, for garnish

**BEEF TENDERLOIN IS OUR FAVORITE** special-occasion dinner. It is known as the king of cuts, the most tender muscle on a steer, so we save this super-premium meat for a big family holiday gathering or a milestone celebration. When tenderloin is cut into steaks, it becomes filet mignon. For roasting, seek out a center cut since the diameter is more consistent throughout the entire roast. Also, make sure the tenderloin is trimmed of fat and silver skin or extra membrane prior to cooking (see page 148). It's remarkably easy to roast this beautiful piece of meat to perfection (just don't overcook it!), and it looks stunning sliced on a platter with the rich and savory sauce over the top. It is equally as delicious served with chimichurri sauce (page 174) or Italian salsa verde (page 173). And for a truly special presentation, pair it with a side of the Hasselback potatoes (page 201).

# BEEF TENDERLOIN <u>WITH</u> CARAMELIZED ONION– RED WINE SAUCE

*Makes 6 servings*

In a small bowl, stir together the olive oil, garlic, spice rub, and thyme. Place the tenderloin on a baking sheet and rub the herb mixture all over. Using kitchen string, tie the roast about every 1½ inches (this will help it hold its shape while roasting). Cover and set aside at room temperature for 1 hour or refrigerate up to overnight; if refrigerated, let stand at room temperature for 1 hour before cooking.

Preheat the oven to 425 degrees F. Place a wire rack in a shallow roasting pan just large enough to hold the tenderloin. Roast until deeply browned and an instant-read thermometer inserted into the center of the roast registers about 125 degrees F for medium-rare, about 45 minutes. Remove the pan from the oven and transfer the tenderloin to a cutting board. Tent loosely with aluminum foil and let rest for 15 to 30 minutes.

Meanwhile, make the sauce. In a large skillet over medium heat, melt 2 tablespoons of the butter. Add the onions and a big pinch of salt and cook, stirring occasionally, until golden and caramelized, 15 to 20 minutes (reduce the heat slightly if they start to brown too quickly). Add the wine, stock, and thyme, and increase the heat to medium-high. Boil the mixture until the liquid reduces by half, about 10 minutes (reduce the heat to medium if the mixture is cooking too rapidly). Stir in the balsamic and sugar and continue to cook for about 1 minute longer. Cover and set aside to keep warm.

**FOR THE BEEF**

2 tablespoons extra-virgin olive oil

3 cloves garlic, minced

1 tablespoon M5 Spice Rub (see page 127), or 1 tablespoon kosher salt and 1 teaspoon freshly ground black pepper

2 teaspoons minced fresh thyme leaves

3-pound center-cut beef tenderloin roast, trimmed of silver skin

**FOR THE SAUCE**

6 tablespoons unsalted butter, divided

2 large yellow onions, halved and thinly sliced

Kosher salt and freshly ground black pepper

2 cups full-bodied red wine

1 cup low-sodium beef stock

3 sprigs fresh thyme

1 tablespoon balsamic vinegar

2 teaspoons packed light brown sugar

When ready to serve, remove the thyme sprigs from the sauce. Reheat over medium-low, then whisk in the remaining 4 table-spoons butter, 1 tablespoon at a time, until emulsified. Remove from the heat, stir in any juices from the cutting board, and season with salt and pepper.

Cut the tenderloin across the grain into thick slices, top with the warm sauce, and serve at once.

# M5 SPICE RUB

After I found myself making the same mix of good-quality salt, freshly ground pepper, and high-end spices for so many recipes, I decided to create a custom spice blend for our customers' convenience too. We use the best possible ingredients: coarse Maldon sea salt, Malabar black peppercorns, organic dried thyme and rosemary, and high-quality red pepper flakes. Starting with premium spices can make a world of difference. This rub is a great seasoning for steaks or chops or anything that's going on the grill, and a perfect addition to roasts that will be braised in the slow cooker. It gives soups or stews a real kick and is also delicious sprinkled on morning eggs or avocado toast. To make your own, in a small bowl stir together 3 tablespoons kosher salt, 2 tablespoons crushed red pepper flakes, 1 tablespoon dried rosemary, 1 tablespoon dried thyme, 2 teaspoons flaky sea salt (preferably Maldon), ¼ teaspoon freshly ground black pepper, and ¼ teaspoon garlic powder. This makes about ½ cup spice rub, which can be stored in an airtight container for up to six months.

Pork

**W**HILE RAISING PIGS IS REWARDING, it's not an easy task. Breeding and farrowing piglets can be a challenge that requires careful attention. Unlike cattle and sheep, who only have one breeding season annually, new litters of piglets are born throughout the year. To make things easier, we built a classic red barn, where our momma pigs have their piglets in roomy individual stalls with a heat lamp for the babies and a cozy bed of straw for the mommas.

We let pigs be pigs. They spend their days out on the pasture, which is remarkably rare for market hogs in the US. Less than 5 percent of pork available in supermarkets is raised outdoors in the dirt. Our hogs roam the green grass pastures, mud wallows, and wild pond area we have dedicated just for them. They have insulated huts for sleeping, to provide shelter from the sun, and to keep them warm in the winter—they certainly live a great life.

We feed the pigs a custom mix of non-GMO protein and nutrients made especially for each hog age group. Gestating pigs get one ration while weaned piglets or growing hogs get another. We tend to avoid throwing scraps to them because it's hard to control what might be in the scraps or how that food was grown. But the pigs do love an apple core shared by one of the girls or some leftover garden veggies at the end of the season.

At Five Marys, we raise Berkshire pigs because we believe they produce some of the finest meat. Berkshire pork has optimal fat and marbling—not too much and not too little—and the meat is flavorful and tender. It's a great heritage breed and provides a super-quality product for our customers.

Our bacon is hands down our bestselling pork product. It's uncured without added nitrates and cut thick. When you start with well-raised pork, you get great bacon. It's always a treat to cook up our own bacon—we can't keep it in stock and try to save it for our customers. But when we do get a pound that isn't quite packaged right it goes into the family pile and everyone gets excited when I fry it up in our cast-iron skillet. So excited that we often eat it hot, right out of the pan! If there is any left, Brian loves it stacked in a summer BLT on homemade sourdough with thick slices of garden tomatoes.

The girls' favorite, and our other bestselling cut of pork, are bone-in pork chops. They love them served with warm, freshly made applesauce, which is easier to prepare than you might think. But I love a good pork roast, slowly braised in the oven or slow cooker, so that it's fall-apart tender. It's my go-to slow-cooker cut to feed a crowd for a big family get-together weekend.

**WITH A SEASONED CHILI RUB** and a sweet-smoky corn and jalapeño salsa, these pork chops pack a ton of flavor and kick. You might think that thin-cut pork chops would dry out quickly, but if you flash-grill them over high heat, the high temperature seals in the juices. Because they cook so fast, you can't beat this for a weeknight dinner. Serve these pork chops with sweet potato fries (page 207) or roasted cauliflower (page 189) to round out the meal.

# CHILI-RUBBED PORK CHOPS <u>WITH</u> CHARRED-CORN SALSA

*Makes 6 servings*

Prepare a grill for direct grilling over medium-high heat (about 450 degrees F). Lay the pork chops on a baking sheet in an even layer. In a small bowl, stir together the olive oil, garlic, chili powder, salt, paprika, and oregano to form a paste. Spread the paste evenly over both sides of the pork chops. Set aside at room temperature for up to 30 minutes.

To make the salsa, brush the corn and onion slices with olive oil and season with salt and pepper. Grill over direct heat, turning once, until tender and slightly charred, about 5 minutes for the onion and 7 minutes for the corn. Transfer to a cutting board. Cut the corn from the cob and finely chop the onion.

Combine the corn and onion in a medium bowl and add the cilantro, jalapeño, lime juice, and 1 teaspoon olive oil. Season with salt and pepper and set aside.

Grill the pork chops over direct heat with the lid closed until nicely grill-marked on one side, 2 to 3 minutes. Turn and cook 1 or 2 minutes longer, until the chops are cooked through but still juicy. Transfer to a platter and let rest for a few minutes, then spoon the salsa over the top, garnish with cilantro, and serve.

**FOR THE PORK**

6 (4-ounce, ¼-inch-thick) bone-in center-cut pork chops
3 tablespoons extra-virgin olive oil
2 cloves garlic, minced
1 tablespoon chili powder
1½ teaspoons kosher salt
1 teaspoon sweet paprika
1 teaspoon dried oregano

**FOR THE SALSA**

2 large ears fresh corn, shucked
2 (½-inch-thick) slices red onion
Extra-virgin olive oil
Kosher salt and freshly ground black pepper
¼ cup finely chopped fresh cilantro leaves, plus extra leaves or sprigs for garnish
1 small jalapeño, seeded and minced
Juice of 1 medium lime (about 2 tablespoons)

PORK

THIS IS THE MOST-REQUESTED DINNER in our family. The girls usually ask for it to be their birthday meal because they love pairing pork chops with warm applesauce. Brining is a great way to infuse flavor and lots of juiciness—use this brine as a starting point, then add aromatics like black peppercorns, orange peels, garlic cloves, fresh sage, or juniper berries to play around and find what you like best. You can use any thick bone-in chop, be it a rib chop or loin (T-bone/porterhouse) chop.

# BRINED PORK CHOPS
# WITH APPLESAUCE

*Makes 6 servings*

Put the pork chops in a baking dish just large enough to hold them in a single layer. In a large bowl, stir together the salt and 8 cups cold water until the salt dissolves. Pour it over the chops, cover, and refrigerate for at least 2 and up to 10 hours.

To make the applesauce, peel and core the apples, then chop into roughly 1-inch pieces. Put the apples in a medium saucepan or Dutch oven and add the water, cinnamon sticks, lemon juice, and salt and stir to combine. Cover and bring to a boil over medium-high heat, then reduce the heat to medium-low and simmer, uncovered and stirring occasionally, until the apples are very soft, about 30 minutes (depending on the type of apples you use). If the mixture starts to dry out, add ¼ cup more water.

Remove the cinnamon sticks. For a chunky sauce, smash the apples with a potato masher; for a smoother sauce, puree the mixture with an immersion blender or blend in batches in a food processor or blender. If the sauce is too thick, add a little more water. If it's not sweet enough, you can always add a little brown sugar. You should have about 2 cups of applesauce. Let cool completely, then store in an airtight container in the refrigerator for up to 1 week.

About 1 hour before cooking the pork chops, remove them from the brine and place on a baking sheet, then pat dry with a paper towel. Prepare a grill for direct cooking over medium heat (about 400 degrees F). Brush the grates clean.

**FOR THE PORK**
6 (10- to 12-ounce, 1-inch-thick) bone-in pork rib or loin chops
½ cup kosher salt

**FOR THE APPLESAUCE**
2 to 2½ pounds apples, such as McIntosh, Golden Delicious, Fuji, Jonagold, or a combination
½ cup water
2 cinnamon sticks, or ½ teaspoon ground cinnamon
Juice of ½ large lemon (about 2 tablespoons)
¼ teaspoon kosher salt

Grill the chops, turning and rotating them a few times so they cook evenly, until nicely grill-marked and an instant-read thermometer reads 135 degrees F, 10 to 13 minutes. The pork should be barely pink in the middle—be careful not to overcook.

Transfer the chops to a cutting board or platter, cover loosely with aluminum foil, and let rest for about 10 minutes. Serve with plenty of applesauce.

## APPLES FOR APPLESAUCE

Fresh applesauce is a big hit at both our family table and at our fall Camp retreats, where we often make it in a cast-iron Dutch oven, but at home I love to make it in the Instant Pot. Simply throw in any cored apples that are slightly past their prime, skin and all, and the sauce is ready in 15 minutes.

We use a mix of local, seasonal apples for the best flavor, and you can't get much more local than the productive apple trees at our guesthouse in town. When all those apples ripen at once, we are always looking for a good way to use them up.

Choosing the best varieties depends on how you like your sauce: apples that hold their shape (like Gravenstein and Granny Smith) yield chunkier sauce, while those that break down more easily (like McIntosh and Cortland) result in a smoother sauce. I like to use a mixture of sweet and more tart varieties to balance the flavor and sweetness. We never add sugar to our applesauce—we let the fruit do the sweetening—but cinnamon or a little ginger is always nice.

ROASTING FRESH TOMATOES INTENSIFIES THEIR flavor, so this sauce is still a winner even if you don't have straight-from-the-vine summer tomatoes. Though if you do, this is an excellent recipe for using up that bounty—especially the tomatoes that are overripe or starting to turn. When I have way more than I know what to do with, I like to make a double batch of this sauce and freeze the extra. The balsamic vinegar amps up the umami factor, and the roasted garlic adds a sweet, silky undertone. I think these saucy meatballs are delicious over a big pile of garlicky sautéed greens, but Brian and the girls always want spaghetti. We usually comprise and have both!

# PORK-AND-RICOTTA MEATBALLS <u>WITH</u> ROASTED GARDEN TOMATO SAUCE

*Makes 6 servings*

To make the tomato sauce, position two oven racks evenly in the oven and preheat to 400 degrees F. Brush two large rimmed baking sheets with olive oil. Spread the tomatoes in an even layer, dividing them evenly among the baking sheets. Drizzle with olive oil, then sprinkle with salt. Place the garlic cloves in the center of one of the baking sheets. Cook until the tomatoes are fragrant and starting to brown, rotating the baking sheets once or twice, about 40 minutes. Check the tomatoes every so often to make sure they aren't burning; if they start to brown too quickly, rotate them on the sheet.

When cool enough to handle, squeeze the softened garlic out of their skins (discard the skins) into a blender. In batches, transfer the tomatoes to the blender and blend until smooth. (If you like, push the tomatoes through a mesh sieve to remove the skin and seeds first; alternatively, run the them through a food mill). Pour the sauce into a large saucepan and stir in the balsamic. Taste and adjust the seasoning with more balsamic and salt, then set aside. The sauce can be cooled completely and stored in an airtight container in the refrigerator for up to 1 week or in the freezer for up to 1 month.

➡

**FOR THE TOMATO SAUCE**
Extra-virgin olive oil
4 pounds fresh ripe tomatoes, thickly sliced
Kosher salt
6 cloves garlic, whole and unpeeled
1 teaspoon balsamic vinegar, plus more if needed

**FOR THE MEATBALLS**
1 pound ground pork
1 pound ground beef, preferably chuck or sirloin
1 cup (about 8 ounces) ricotta cheese
⅓ cup grated Parmesan cheese, plus more for garnish
½ small yellow onion, finely chopped (about ⅓ cup)
1 large egg, lightly beaten
1 teaspoon Italian seasoning
½ teaspoon ground fennel
1 teaspoon kosher salt
½ teaspoon freshly ground black pepper
Chopped fresh basil leaves, for garnish

To make the meatballs, increase the oven temperature to 450 degrees F. Brush a clean rimmed baking sheet with olive oil. In a large bowl add the pork, beef, ricotta, Parmesan, onion, egg, Italian seasoning, ground fennel, salt, and pepper. Mix gently with your hands until combined. Shape into meatballs, each about 2 inches in diameter. You should have about 28 meatballs. Space the meatballs evenly on the baking sheet and bake until cooked through and well browned on one side, about 20 minutes.

Using a silicone spatula, loosen the meatballs from the pan and add them to the sauce. Bring to a gentle simmer over medium heat for about 20 minutes, gently moving the meatballs around occasionally. Transfer to a wide serving bowl and garnish with more Parmesan and the basil.

# MEATBALL VARIATION

Meatballs are such a versatile and family-friendly meal, whether you serve them on their own, top a plate of pasta with them, or get creative! This recipe is a great jumping-off point. You can make it as written, use all beef or all pork, or even swap it out for lamb (there's another great recipe for lamb meatballs on page 167). Turn these into sandwiches by stuffing the meatballs into hoagie rolls and topping with provolone cheese and plenty of the sauce, or make cute little meatball sliders. Use this method for making the meatballs, but mix it up with different spices and sauces to create an entirely new dish. Pork meatballs made with plenty of ground cumin are great in a tomatillo sauce, and beef meatballs mixed with chopped cilantro and a little hoisin sauce would be amazing in a hearty ramen noodle soup.

WHENEVER I NEED TO FEED a crowd, like when we head out of town to a rodeo week-end, I always make a bunch of pulled pork because it's so easy when you use a slow cooker. It's good straight from the pot with creamy coleslaw, or loaded onto just about everything: sandwiches, tacos, nachos (page 69), salads—or Brian's favorite, breakfast burritos (page 26). Pork shoulder roasts are the classic cut for pulled pork, but you can also use leg or arm roasts for equally tender shreddable meat. The Ranch-Barbecue Sauce is worth the effort, but you can also just use any favorite sauce.

# SLOW-COOKER PULLED PORK SANDWICHES

*Makes 10 to 12 servings*

Pat the pork butt dry and rub all over with the spice rub. Place the pork in a 6- to 8-quart slow cooker.

Halve the oranges and squeeze most of the juice into the slow cooker, then cut each half into quarters and toss them in too. Add the cider, onion, and garlic. Cover and cook on low for 10 hours or high for 8 hours.

Transfer the pork to a cutting board. When cool enough to handle, shred the pork with two dinner forks, removing and discarding the bone and any big pieces of fat or gristle. Strain the cooking juices through a fine-mesh sieve into a bowl, discarding any solids. Using a large metal spoon, skim off as much fat from the surface of the liquid as possible. Return the meat and juices to the slow cooker and cook on low until the meat is warm, very tender, and has absorbed some of the liquid, about 1 hour.

Pile the pork on the bottom of each toasted bun, then drizzle with the sauce. Pile the coleslaw on top of the meat (or on the side). Top the sandwiches with the remaining bun halves and serve right away.

Leftover pulled pork can be cooled completely and stored in an air-tight container in the refrigerator for up to 4 days or in the freezer for up to 1 month.

1 (5- to 6-pound) bone-in pork shoulder butt

1½ tablespoons M5 Spice Rub (see page 127), or kosher salt and freshly ground black pepper

2 medium oranges

1 cup apple cider or water

1 medium yellow onion, chopped

3 cloves garlic, peeled and smashed

10 to 12 burger buns, split and toasted

3 to 4 cups barbecue sauce, homemade (page 147) or store-bought

Creamy Coleslaw (page 191)

PORK

THIS RAGÙ IS A HAPPY marriage of pulled pork and Bolognese. You'd never know that such a luxurious sauce could be as effortless as a quick sauté and then a hands-off braise in the slow cooker. It's so simple! My family loves the ragù over fresh pasta, but it's equally at home topping bowls of creamy polenta (page 200). I always make a big batch of the sauce and store it in mason jars in the fridge to have an easy dinner option for pastas or lasagna over a week or two.

# SHREDDED PORK RAGÙ WITH PASTA

*Makes 6 servings with leftover sauce*

To make the ragù, in a deep wide skillet over medium-high heat, cook the bacon, stirring, until it renders its fat and starts to brown, 4 to 5 minutes. You need a few tablespoons of fat in the pan, so pour off a little if it's too much or add the olive oil if the bacon doesn't render enough. Add the onion, carrots, celery, garlic, and salt and cook, stirring, until the vegetables soften, about 5 minutes. Stir in the tomato paste, then add the tomatoes with juices and the Italian seasoning, and stir to mix well. Bring to a simmer, then remove from the heat. Transfer the tomato mixture to a 6- to 8-quart slow cooker and add the pork, submerging it in the sauce. Cover and cook on low for 8 hours. The pork should be very tender.

Using a large metal spoon, skim as much fat as you can from the surface of the sauce. Transfer the pork to a cutting board. Using two forks, shred the pork, removing any large pieces of fat. Return the shredded pork to the sauce, cover, and cook on high for 15 minutes to warm through. You should have about 10 cups of ragù, but you only need about half for this recipe; the remainder can be saved for another meal. Cool unused ragù completely and store it in an airtight container in the refrigerator for up to 3 days or in the freezer for up to 3 months.

Bring a large pot three-quarters full of salted water to a boil over high heat. Add the pasta and cook until al dente, about 5 minutes or according to package directions. Drain and transfer to a large shallow serving bowl.

Add enough warm ragù to the pasta to cover it well and toss to coat. Top with more sauce, then garnish with parsley and Parmesan and serve.

½ pound thick-cut smoked bacon, finely chopped

1 tablespoon extra-virgin olive oil (optional)

1 large yellow onion, finely chopped

2 medium carrots, peeled and finely chopped

2 stalks celery, finely chopped

4 large cloves garlic, minced

1 teaspoon kosher salt

¼ cup tomato paste

1 (28-ounce) can crushed tomatoes

1 (15-ounce) can diced tomatoes

1 tablespoon Italian seasoning

3 pounds boneless pork shoulder, trimmed of excess fat and cut into 4 equal pieces

2 pounds fresh fettuccine or pasta of choice, or 1½ pounds dried

¼ cup chopped fresh flat-leaf parsley leaves, for garnish

Grated Parmesan cheese, for garnish

THESE ARE SPECIAL-OCCASION RIBS THAT take a bit of time to make, but I think they are worth it. You can make the rub and the sauce up to a week in advance, and most of the cooking is hands-off; you just need to stick around to make sure the grill temperature stays consistent and occasionally stoke the fire. It is so satisfying to set these tender smoky ribs out and have your family ask for more. Tess has even been known to steal the bones off of our plates and find any bit of meat that's left on them! They are fantastic with Rustic Baked Beans (page 208) and Creamy Coleslaw (page 191).

# SMOKED SPARERIBS <u>WITH</u> RANCH-BARBECUE SAUCE

*Makes 6 to 8 servings*

To make the rub, in a small bowl, whisk together all the ingredients until well combined.

Place the rib racks on a large rimmed baking sheet, bone side up. If the ribs still have silver skin membrane attached, use a dinner knife to pry it up on one corner, then, using a paper towel, grab the membrane and gently pull it off. Trim any excess fat from the ribs. Coat the racks all over with the spice rub, especially the meatier side. Cover and refrigerate for at least 1 hour or up to overnight.

Remove the ribs from the refrigerator while you prepare a water smoker or grill for indirect cooking over very low heat (225 to 250 degrees F; see page 150). Cover the grill and let it come to temperature. If using wood chips, drain them. Add the wood chips or chunks to the grill. Replace the cooking grate and brush clean. Place the ribs, meaty side up, on the cooking grate over indirect heat. Smoke with the lid closed until the ribs are very tender, about 5 hours. Change the position of each rib rack about once an hour, turning and rotating them so they cook evenly. Keep a close eye on the temperature, and if it begins to drop, add a few more pieces of charcoal (you can also light half a chimney on a heatproof surface first).

While the ribs smoke, make the sauce. In a medium saucepan over medium heat, warm the oil. Add the onion and a pinch of salt and cook, stirring, until the onion softens and starts to brown, about 7 minutes. Stir in the ketchup, beer, vinegar, Worcestershire, sugar, molasses, 1 teaspoon salt, black pepper, and red pepper flakes. Bring the ingredients to a simmer, then reduce the heat to low and cook, stirring occasionally, until the flavors meld, about 15 minutes.

**FOR THE RUB**
2 tablespoons chili powder
1 tablespoon ancho chili powder
1 tablespoon sweet paprika
1 tablespoon ground cumin
1 tablespoon packed light brown sugar
1 tablespoon kosher salt
1 teaspoon freshly ground black pepper

**FOR THE RIBS**
2 racks pork spareribs (about 6 pounds total)
3 or 4 handfuls of wood chips, soaked for 30 minutes, or 4 wood chunks, optional (see page 150)

**FOR THE SAUCE**
2 tablespoons canola oil
1 small red onion, finely chopped
Kosher salt
2 cups ketchup
1 (12-ounce) bottle porter ale
½ cup apple cider vinegar
2 tablespoons Worcestershire sauce
2 tablespoons packed light brown sugar
1 tablespoon dark molasses (not blackstrap)
½ teaspoon freshly ground black pepper
½ teaspoon red pepper flakes

➡

PORK

Use an immersion blender or transfer the sauce to a blender and blend until pureed (or leave as is if you prefer a chunkier sauce). Season with more salt, vinegar, or red pepper flakes if you like. You should have about 4 cups of sauce. (The sauce can be made up to 1 week in advance; cool completely and store in an airtight container in the refrigerator.)

The ribs are done when the meat is very tender, has pulled back from the bones, and tears away easily when a rack is lifted with tongs. Brush the racks on both sides with a thick, even layer of sauce. Cover the grill and continue to cook until crisp and sticky, about 10 minutes. Brush with more sauce, then transfer to a cutting board. Let rest for about 5 minutes before cutting each rack into individual ribs. Serve right away with the remaining sauce on the side.

# REMOVING SILVER SKIN

Silver skin is a membrane found on certain cuts of meat, such as pork tenderloin and pork and beef ribs. It looks like a silvery swath on the surface of the meat, hence the name. It doesn't break down when you cook the meat and can be tough to chew, so it's always best to remove it before cooking. To remove the silver skin, locate the membrane on the outside of the meat; it's easier to see if you turn the meat under light to look for the reflection. Insert a boning knife or another thin, sharp knife under the silver skin toward the middle of the strip. Use the knife blade to get under the skin, all the way to the opposite side of the silver skin strip. Angle the blade of your knife upward to minimize nicking the meat as much as possible. Move the knife blade toward one edge of the silver skin as it releases from the meat. Repeat on the other side of the silver skin to remove the entire strip, then discard.

# SETTING UP YOUR GRILL FOR SMOKING

Smoking meats over a low, slow fire infuses them with intense flavor. My favorite kind of wood for smoking ribs is oak, but you can use applewood or hickory instead. If you use wood chips, be sure to soak them in water for at least 30 minutes well in advance so they don't burn too quickly; alternatively, use wood chunks, which you don't have to soak (not advised for a gas grill).

You can use any kind of grill, but we tend to use a charcoal water smoker or a charcoal grill at the ranch. If using a charcoal water smoker, depending on its size, light a half to a full chimney of charcoal. When gray with ash, add it to the bottom of the smoker, then suspend the water bowl above the charcoal and fill it three-quarters full with water. Add the wood directly on the coals once the grill comes to temperature and replace the cooking grate.

If using a charcoal grill, position the coals to one side, leaving about two-thirds of the grill free for cooking. Place a drip pan in the center and fill halfway with water. Add the wood directly on the coals once the grill comes to temperature and replace the cooking grate.

Using a gas grill is even easier. Just set it up for indirect low heat, and once it comes to temperature, add the wood chips (don't use chunks) to the smoker box. If your grill doesn't have a smoker box, create one! Place the wood chips in a small foil pan, cover tightly with aluminum foil, then poke holes in the top with a paring knife. Put in on the grill grate above the fire and you've got yourself a smoker.

SWEET, SPICY, SALTY, AND SAVORY: the perfectly balanced sauce for these ribs packs a real punch and delivers lots of umami. You can make them as spicy as you want by adding more (or less) sriracha. This recipe offers a great alternative method for cooking ribs without having to fire up a smoker or grill—you just cook them low and slow in the oven until tender and deeply glazed. They are fantastic as an appetizer on their own, or you can serve them as a main dish along with steamed rice and roasted veggies (we like asparagus).

# SWEET-AND-SPICY BABY BACK RIBS

*Makes 6 to 8 servings*

In a small bowl, stir together the five-spice, sugar, salt, and pepper. Season both rib racks all over with the rub. Set aside at room temperature while the oven preheats, or wrap in plastic wrap and refrigerate overnight. (If refrigerated, let sit at room temperature for 1 hour before cooking.)

Preheat the oven to 300 degrees F. Line a large rimmed baking sheet with aluminum foil, then set a wire rack on top. Lay the rib racks on the wire rack, meaty side up. Wrap the baking sheet with foil and roast for 2 hours. Remove the foil (set aside for later) and roast for 30 minutes longer.

While the ribs are roasting, make the sauce. In a small saucepan over medium-low heat, warm the oil. Add the garlic and ginger and cook, stirring, until fragrant, about 2 minutes. Stir in the remaining sauce ingredients. Bring the mixture to a boil, stirring, then remove from the heat.

After the ribs have cooked for 2½ hours, brush them all over with about two-thirds of the sauce. Continue to roast, uncovered, until the ribs are tender but not falling apart, 30 to 60 minutes more. Remove from the oven, brush with the remaining sauce, and wrap the pan in foil again. Let rest for 15 to 30 minutes.

To serve, cut the ribs between the bones and transfer to a serving platter, then garnish with the green onions and cilantro.

**FOR THE RIBS**
1 tablespoon Chinese five-spice powder
1 tablespoon packed dark brown sugar
1 tablespoon kosher salt
2 teaspoons freshly ground black pepper
2 racks baby back ribs (about 5 pounds total), trimmed of silver skin (see page 148)

**FOR THE SAUCE**
1 tablespoon canola oil
3 cloves garlic, minced
1 tablespoon packed peeled and grated fresh ginger
¼ cup hoisin sauce
¼ cup soy sauce
2 tablespoons packed dark brown sugar
1 tablespoon unseasoned rice vinegar
1 tablespoon sriracha or other hot sauce
1 teaspoon toasted sesame oil
½ teaspoon red pepper flakes
½ teaspoon freshly ground black pepper
¼ teaspoon ground cinnamon

**FOR GARNISH**
4 green onions (white and green parts), chopped
½ cup chopped fresh cilantro leaves

PORK

153

THIS IS SUCH A GREAT WAY to cook pork leg or arm roasts, which are a lot like pork shoulder, rendering them fall-apart tender. Like my pulled pork, I make this in the slow cooker because it's so easy. I'll stack as many roasts in there as will fit, which makes plenty to feed a crowd or have leftovers for a few more meals. The balance of flavors in this dish are phenomenal—sweet honey, spicy ginger, and lots of bright citrus—and the pork is perfect for topping a bowl of steamed rice or Chinese egg noodles. Add some steamed baby bok choy or sautéed sugar snap peas and dinner is ready! Leftovers are delicious tucked into a sandwich or tossed in a salad.

# HONEY–GINGER BRAISED PORK RICE BOWLS

*Makes 6 to 8 servings*

Pat the pork dry and season it all over with salt and pepper. Transfer to a 6- to 8-quart slow cooker.

In a small saucepan over medium heat, combine the soy sauce, honey, sugar, citrus zest and juices, garlic, and ginger and bring to a simmer, stirring with a whisk, until the sugar dissolves and the mixture is combined. Pour over the pork, cover, and cook on low for 10 hours or high for 8 hours.

Transfer the pork to a cutting board. When cool enough to handle, shred the pork with two forks, removing and discarding the bone and any large pieces of fat or gristle. Strain the cooking juices through a fine-mesh sieve into a bowl, discarding any solids. Using a large metal spoon, skim off as much fat from the surface of the liquid as possible. Return the meat and juices to the slow cooker and cook on low until the meat is warm, very tender, and has absorbed some of the liquid, about 1 hour longer.

To serve, top bowls of rice with the pork and cooking juices, then garnish with the green onions.

5 to 6 pounds bone-in pork leg or arm roasts (about 2), or 1 pork shoulder roast, trimmed of excess fat

Kosher salt and freshly ground black pepper

¼ cup soy sauce

¼ cup honey

¼ cup packed light brown sugar

Zest and juice of 1 medium orange

Juice of 2 medium limes (about 4 tablespoons)

3 cloves garlic, minced

1 tablespoon peeled and grated fresh ginger

Hot steamed white or brown rice, for serving

4 green onions (white and green parts), thinly sliced, for garnish

WRAPPING AN ENTIRE PORK TENDERLOIN with smoky bacon that's been woven into a lattice takes the cut to an entirely new level. This is a fun way to add some flair and impress your guests. Rubbing the pork with a simple mustardy paste (which can be done the day before) pumps up the flavor. I often use my cast-iron pan to roast meat in the oven, and it's particularly useful in this recipe because it creates a great crust and helps brown the bacon. Once the tenderloin is nearly ready, I glaze it with honey to give it that little bit of sweetness pork loves.

# BACON-WRAPPED PORK TENDERLOIN

*Makes 6 to 8 servings*

In a small bowl, stir together the mustard, paprika, salt, and pepper. Rub the pork tenderloins evenly all over with the mixture. Set aside for up to 30 minutes at room temperature, or cover and refrigerate for up to overnight.

Preheat the oven to 425 degrees F.

For each tenderloin, lay 4 or 5 bacon strips (depending on how wide they are; the width should fit the tenderloin) on a piece of parchment parallel to each other and just touching. To weave the lattice, fold every other strip halfway back onto itself. Lay 1 strip of bacon perpendicular over the strips, snug against the folds, then unfold the strips again. Next, fold back the opposite strips, place another bacon strip parallel to the first weave, then unfold the perpendicular strips again. Repeat until you have woven in 4 or 5 strips. Adjust the bacon to make sure the strips are snug.

Lay one tenderloin on the end of the bacon lattice closest to you and fold over the thin flap so it fits the width of the bacon. Gently, using the parchment to help you, roll the bacon snugly around the tenderloin, positioning it seam side down. Repeat with the second tenderloin.

Place the tenderloins seam side down in a large cast-iron skillet or other heavy ovenproof pan, making sure the tenderloins are separated by a few inches. Adjust the bacon so it is snug against the tenderloin. Transfer to the oven. Roast until the bacon is browned and crisp and the tenderloin is cooked to the preferred doneness, 30 to 35 minutes for medium (135 degrees F). About 5 minutes before the pork is done, brush some of the honey all over the tops and sides of the tenderloins to form a glaze.

Remove from the oven, brush with a little more honey, then let rest in the pan for 10 minutes. Carefully transfer the tenderloins to a cutting board, carve into thick slices, and serve.

2 tablespoons whole-grain Dijon or brown mustard

1 teaspoon sweet paprika

1 teaspoon kosher salt

½ teaspoon freshly ground black pepper

2 (1-pound) pork tenderloins, trimmed of silver skin (see page 148)

16 to 20 thin-cut slices bacon (1¼ to 1½ pounds)

3 tablespoons honey, warmed

Lamb

**W**HEN SOMEONE TELLS ME THEY like steak or pork but don't eat lamb, I take it as a personal challenge. For most, it's because they've only tried mediocre lamb that has a very strong flavor or hasn't been cooked correctly. Much of the lamb sold in the United States is imported and raised to grow quickly, whereas slow-growing heritage lamb is second to none in delicate flavor and tenderness.

We raise Navajo-Churro sheep, a heritage breed that is known as the "chef's choice" for this very reason. It's mild but extremely flavorful, not like the strong and gamey lamb or mutton our parents or grandparents may have grown up eating, covered in mint jelly to mask the unpleasantly bold taste. Navajo-Churro are a hearty, wild breed that do really well in the colder temperatures that we get at the ranch. They are also beautiful, so we save and sell the tanned hides, pelts, and skulls; it's another way to honor our animals.

The sheep and lambs graze on pasture grasses and run free in their pastures during the day, but they are the easiest prey on the ranch, so we go to great lengths to keep them as safe as possible by moving the flock into the barn area near the house every night, where predators are much less likely to get them. We help guide them for a few weeks every spring, but before long the sheep and lambs learn to do it on their own without us having to herd them in! Of course, the dogs are extra protective of our herd as well and work hard to keep them safe (see page 170).

Lamb chops and ground lamb are our most popular cuts, and they are the two I recommend people try first if they are unsure about lamb. I've lost count of how many friends, family members, and visitors to the ranch Brian and I have converted just by feeding them a great lamb burger or some delicious grilled chops. My personal favorite, though, is a deboned leg of lamb, cut into meaty steaks, grilled to perfection, and served with vibrant, fresh chimichurri sauce. And the girls love our spicy merguez sausage, especially in baked eggs. I'd encourage anyone who hasn't tried it recently to experiment with well-raised American lamb—you won't be disappointed!

AT THE BURGERHOUSE, WE MAKE full-size lamb burgers, but at home our girls love these mini sliders. I also like serving them as appetizers when we are entertaining up at Camp. The tangy-sweet chutney is a natural partner to lamb, but it's also terrific with grilled pork chops. If you want a bit of kick, add some cayenne to the chutney along with the other spices. Use dinner rolls in a pinch if you can't find slider buns. If you'd rather do full-size burgers, simply divide the meat into only six portions and increase the cooking time by a few minutes. These are also really nice with chimichurri (page 174).

# GRILLED LAMB SLIDERS WITH TOMATO CHUTNEY AND HAVARTI

*Makes 12 sliders*

To make the chutney, in a medium saucepan over medium-low heat, warm the olive oil. Add the mustard seeds, swirl the pan, then add the onion and garlic. Cook, stirring, until the onion softens, about 5 minutes. Stir in the sugar, vinegar, cinnamon stick, ginger, and 1 teaspoon salt, then add the tomatoes. Simmer, stirring often, until the mixture thickens, about 15 minutes. Remove from the heat and stir in the lemon juice. Season with more salt if needed. Let cool completely. You should have about 1 cup of chutney. The chutney can be made up to 1 week in advance and stored in an airtight container in the refrigerator.

To make the sliders, in a large bowl and using your hands, gently mix together the lamb, salt, coriander, pepper, and cumin until well combined. Divide the mixture into 12 equal portions (each about 2 ounces), roll each piece into a ball, then flatten into a patty ½ inch thick. Place on a large rimmed baking sheet.

Spread the cut sides of each bun lightly with the butter. Heat a large cast-iron griddle or two cast-iron pans (or cook in batches) over medium-high heat, then add the buns, cut sides down. Cook until toasted, about 2 minutes, then transfer to a serving platter. Brush the griddle or pans with the oil. Add the patties, and cook the first side until nicely seared, about 2 minutes. Turn the patties, top each with a piece of cheese, and continue to cook to medium-rare or medium and until the cheese is slightly melted, 1 to 2 minutes longer. Transfer the patties to the bun bottoms. Top each patty with about 1 tablespoon of the chutney, place the top bun on top, and serve at once.

## FOR THE CHUTNEY

2 tablespoons extra-virgin olive oil
1 teaspoon whole yellow mustard seeds
½ medium yellow onion, finely chopped
2 cloves garlic, minced
⅓ cup packed light brown sugar
¼ cup apple cider vinegar
1 cinnamon stick
½ teaspoon ground ginger
Kosher salt
1 (14.5-ounce) can crushed tomatoes
1 teaspoon freshly squeezed lemon juice

## FOR THE SLIDERS

1½ pounds ground lamb
1½ teaspoons kosher salt
1½ teaspoons ground coriander
1½ teaspoons freshly ground black pepper
¾ teaspoon ground cumin
12 slider buns, split
¼ cup unsalted butter, at room temperature
1 tablespoon canola oil
12 slices (about 6 ounces) sliced Havarti cheese

THESE MEDITERRANEAN-INSPIRED MEATBALLS ARE well suited for hot summer days on the ranch, especially with the addition of fresh herbs, a cooling cucumber-yogurt sauce, and the tangy heat of the harissa paste. They are fantastic tucked into thick toasted pitas or served on a bed of lettuce with the sauces drizzled over the top. I also love to serve the meatballs for bigger events or celebrations because they make a great passed appetizer with the tzatziki and harissa on the side for dipping.

# SPICY LAMB MEATBALLS WITH CUCUMBER–MINT TZATZIKI

*Makes 6 servings*

Set a large rimmed baking sheet near your prep station. To make the meatballs, in a large bowl and using your hands, gently mix all of the ingredients except the oil until well combined. Scoop up about 2 tablespoons of the lamb mixture at a time and gently roll into meatballs about 1½ inches in diameter. Transfer to the baking sheet as you finish forming them; you should have about 26 meatballs. Set aside.

Preheat the oven to 225 degrees F. Place a clean rimmed baking sheet in the oven.

To make the tzatziki, shred the cucumber on the large holes of a box grater. Press out as much liquid as possible from the cucumber using paper towels. Transfer to a medium bowl along with the remaining ingredients and stir until well combined. Cover and refrigerate until ready to use.

In a large cast-iron pan over medium heat, working in batches, toast the pita on both sides, then wrap in aluminum foil and keep warm in the oven.

To cook the meatballs, increase the heat to medium-high and add the oil. When hot, add half of the meatballs and cook, turning a few times as the bottoms become richly browned, until cooked through, 8 to 10 minutes. Transfer to the baking sheet in the oven to keep warm while you cook the remaining meatballs; add a little more oil if the pan gets dry.

Arrange the meatballs and warm pitas on a platter, then scatter the mint and cilantro over the meatballs. Serve with bowls of tzatziki and harissa alongside. To assemble, split a pita half, stuff it with 2 or 3 meatballs and some herbs, then top with tzatziki and harissa.

**FOR THE MEATBALLS**
2 pounds ground lamb
¼ cup grated yellow onion
2 cloves garlic, minced
2 tablespoons finely chopped fresh mint leaves
2 tablespoons finely chopped fresh cilantro leaves
1 tablespoon harissa, or 1 teaspoon red pepper flakes
2 teaspoons ground cumin
1½ teaspoons kosher salt
1½ teaspoons freshly ground black pepper
¼ cup vegetable oil, plus more if needed

**FOR THE TZATZIKI**
½ English cucumber
1 cup plain whole-milk Greek yogurt
1 tablespoon freshly squeezed lemon juice
1 tablespoon finely chopped fresh mint leaves
½ teaspoon ground cumin

**FOR SERVING**
6 thick pitas, halved crosswise
⅓ cup chopped fresh mint leaves
⅓ cup chopped fresh cilantro leaves
¼ cup harissa

LAMB LOIN CHOPS MIGHT BE small compared to other cuts, but they are mighty in flavor. This vibrant Moroccan spice rub is a natural partner to the earthy taste of lamb, while the green olive–orange relish provides a satisfying salty-sweet note. Feel free to mix and match the sauces from the other lamb recipes as you like; they are interchangeable depending on what cuts you have on hand and what you are in the mood for that day. I like to serve this with the Herb-Roasted Smasher Potatoes (page 204).

# LAMB LOIN CHOPS WITH GREEN OLIVE–ORANGE RELISH

*Makes 6 servings*

In a small bowl, stir together the cumin, coriander, paprika, cinnamon, salt, and pepper. Put the lamb chops on a baking sheet in a single layer and pat dry with paper towels. Brush the chops all over with a little olive oil. Sprinkle evenly on both sides with the spice mixture. Set aside at room temperature for up to 30 minutes.

To make the relish, in a medium bowl, stir together all the ingredients. Set aside.

In a large cast-iron skillet over medium-high heat, add 2 tablespoons olive oil. When hot, reduce the heat to medium and add the lamb chops. Cook until well browned on the bottom, 4 to 5 minutes. Turn over the chops and cook to the preferred doneness, 4 to 5 minutes longer for medium-rare (about 130 degrees F). Transfer the chops to a serving plate and cover loosely with aluminum foil; let rest for 5 minutes.

Top with the relish and serve at once.

**FOR THE LAMB**
2 teaspoons ground cumin
1 teaspoon ground coriander
1 teaspoon sweet paprika
½ teaspoon ground cinnamon
½ teaspoon kosher salt
½ teaspoon freshly ground
  black pepper
12 (1¼-inch-thick) bone-in lamb
  loin chops (2½ to 3 pounds
  total)
Extra-virgin olive oil

**FOR THE RELISH**
½ cup packed finely chopped
  pitted green olives, preferably
  Lucques or Picholine
¼ cup chopped fresh flat-leaf
  parsley leaves
3 tablespoons extra-virgin
  olive oil
1 tablespoon freshly squeezed
  lemon juice
1 tablespoon freshly squeezed
  orange juice
Finely grated zest of 1 orange
  (about 1 teaspoon)

# GUARDIANS OF THE HERD

Shortly after we moved to the ranch, we got our first livestock guardian dog (LGD), an eighteen-month-old Great Pyrenees named Beauregard. He had already been trained to protect chickens and goats by a young girl as her 4-H project, so we put him in the pasture with the chickens and started getting him used to his new turf, doing things like walking the perimeter fencing with him and not "playing" too much. For the first few days he stayed right there with the chickens, but then he snuck under a fence and started patrolling the sheep, and then the pigs, and then the cattle, and finally the cabin where we slept, circling it at night. They say LGDs protect the most valuable species on a ranch and, in Beau's eyes, that was the girls. Beau, and our other Great Pyrenees, Bitsy, are great with the kids and let them climb all over them, but if a delivery driver or unexpected guest shows up after dark, they jump into action.

While the dogs are part of our family, they aren't pets. They have a job to do on the ranch, which is to protect, guard, and stalk the property all night long. We get many kinds of predators—bears, mountain lions, coyotes, and bobcats—and our LGDs will roam far. A local trapper saw Beau's prints chasing off a bear for six miles! The dogs have even shown up in town five miles down the road and needed to be walked home. After a night out protecting their herds, they will sleep all day, and we often treat them to big meaty bones to thank them for their efforts.

"LAMB LOLLIPOP" IS MY FAVORITE way to describe a lamb rib chop cut from the rack. These tender, mild chops are my girls most-requested dinner, with the exception of pork chops with applesauce (page 134). The Italian-inspired salsa verde is bright and briny, and tastes fantastic paired with any grilled meat, including steak and pork chops.

# GRILLED LAMB LOLLIPOPS WITH SALSA VERDE

*Makes 6 servings*

To make the salsa verde, in the bowl of a food processor, pulse all of the ingredients, including ¼ teaspoon salt and a few grinds of pepper, until well chopped and combined. Scrape down the bowl with a silicone spatula and pulse again. Taste and season with more salt and pepper. Transfer to a small serving bowl and set aside.

Prepare a grill for direct and indirect cooking over high heat (450 to 500 degrees F). Brush the grates clean. Drizzle the lamb with olive oil and season all over with salt and pepper. Grill over direct heat with the lid closed as much as possible, turning once, until cooked to the preferred doneness, about 3 minutes on the first side and 1 to 2 minutes on the second side for medium-rare.

Transfer to a serving plate, spoon some of the salsa verde over the chops, and serve at once.

**FOR THE SALSA VERDE**
1 cup packed chopped fresh parsley leaves
¼ cup chopped fresh basil leaves
½ cup extra-virgin olive oil
2 hard-boiled egg yolks
1 tablespoon capers, rinsed
2 anchovy fillets
1 clove garlic, minced
Juice of ½ medium lemon (about 2 tablespoons)
1 tablespoons red wine vinegar
¼ teaspoon red pepper flakes
Kosher salt and freshly ground black pepper

**FOR THE LAMB**
12 (¾-inch-thick) lamb rib chops (about 2 pounds total), trimmed of excess fat
Extra-virgin olive oil
Kosher salt and freshly ground black pepper

LAMB

ONE OF MY FAVORITE WAYS to prepare leg of lamb is to debone it (see page 176), cut it into thick "steaks" in similar fashion to a tri-tip, and grill the steaks over a hot fire. The meat takes on the char and smoke of the grill, giving the outside a deeply browned, flavorful crust, while the center stays perfectly rosy and moist. Slice it thinly and top it with tangy chimichurri, and you can't go wrong. Chimichurri, a bold herby green sauce, is one of my go-tos because it's not only delicious, it's a breeze to whip together and uses ingredients you likely already have on hand. Terrific on steaks, veggies, eggs, or almost any favorite dish, the chimichurri tastes even better after it's been in the fridge for a few days.

# GRILLED LAMB STEAKS WITH CHIMICHURRI

*Makes 6 servings*

To make the chimichurri, in a medium bowl, stir together all the ingredients until well combined. Alternatively, add the ingredients to a food processor and pulse until chopped and well combined. Season with salt and pepper and set aside.

Debone the leg of lamb and cut it lengthwise into three or four equal portions. Rub the lamb all over with the oil, then season generously with salt and pepper. Set aside at room temperature for up to 30 minutes while you prepare the grill.

Prepare a grill for direct cooking over medium-high heat (about 400 to 450 degrees F). Brush the grates clean. Grill the lamb steaks over direct heat with the lid closed until cooked to the preferred doneness, 10 to 15 minutes for medium-rare (130 degrees F), depending on how thick the steaks are. To ensure they cook evenly, reposition and flip them a few times during cooking. Transfer the lamb to a cutting board, cover loosely with aluminum foil, and let rest for 10 minutes.

Thinly slice the lamb steaks against the grain and arrange on a warm platter. Top with the chimichurri and serve at once.

**FOR THE CHIMICHURRI**
1 cup packed finely chopped fresh flat-leaf parsley leaves (about 1 bunch)
2 tablespoons loosely packed finely chopped fresh oregano
2 cloves garlic, minced
6 tablespoons extra-virgin olive oil
¼ cup red wine vinegar
½ teaspoon red pepper flakes
Kosher salt and freshly ground black pepper

**FOR THE LAMB**
1 (4- to 6-pound) semi-boneless leg of lamb, trimmed of silver skin (see page 148)
1 tablespoon extra-virgin olive oil
Kosher salt and freshly ground black pepper

# DEBONING LEG OF LAMB

A semi-boneless leg of lamb, which we sell at Five Marys, has the lamb shank removed (to be used in other delicious recipes, like the one on page 178), and the hip bone and hinge end of the shank bone removed, leaving the butt end. There's still a bone in there, though, which is ideal to have in place if you are making a whole roasted leg of lamb (page 180) as it will cook more quickly, plus the bone adds flavor, and you can gnaw on it or share with your favorite pup. For lamb steaks or a boneless lamb roast, you'll want to remove the bone. But don't worry: it's easy!

**1.** First, using a very sharp knife (I recommend a boning knife), cut down the length of the leg from one end of the bone to the other, all the way through to the bone and following its contour.

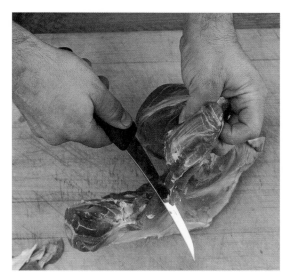

**2.** Carefully cut the meat away from the bone, working as closely as possible to it and running the tip of the knife around and under the bone as you go to loosen the meat.

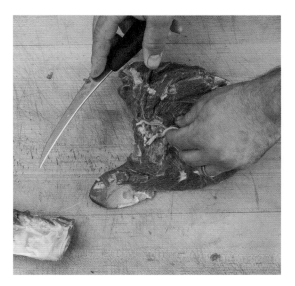

**3.** Remove the bone. Cut away any gristle or connective tissue. Cut the meat length-wise into three or four equal portions, or use the butter-flied boneless leg of lamb for your favorite roast recipe.

LEAN LAMB SHANKS—WHICH ARE cut from the lower leg and can be tough—become meltingly tender and richly flavorful when cooked long and low, either in the oven or a slow cooker. And since lamb pairs beautifully with herbs, tomatoes, and red wine, this sauce is an ideal way to bring them all together. Brian loves to come home during the cold winter months to the aromas of this dish wafting through the cabin.

# BRAISED LAMB SHANKS IN RED WINE SAUCE

*Makes 6 servings*

Preheat the oven to 325 degrees F. Season the lamb shanks all over with salt and pepper. In a large Dutch oven over medium-high heat, warm the olive oil. Working in batches if necessary, add the lamb and sear, turning a few times, until nicely browned all over, about 8 minutes. Transfer the lamb to a plate.

Reduce the heat to medium and add the onion, carrots, and celery to the pot. Cook, stirring to scrape up any browned bits, until softened, about 6 minutes. Add the garlic and cook until fragrant, about 1 minute, then stir in the tomato paste. Stir in the wine, increase the heat to medium-high, and let the mixture come to a boil. Simmer for 2 minutes. Add the stock, tomato sauce, herb sprigs, ½ teaspoon salt, and ¼ teaspoon pepper, and stir to combine. Tuck the lamb shanks into the sauce, submerging them as much as possible. Return the mixture to a boil, then cover and transfer to the oven.

Cook until the lamb shanks are fall-apart tender, stirring every so often, about 2½ hours. Carefully transfer the lamb shanks to a warm serving platter and cover with aluminum foil to keep warm. Discard the herb sprigs.

Skim any fat from the surface of the braising liquid, then bring to a boil over medium-high heat. Reduce the heat to medium and simmer until slightly thickened, 5 to 10 minutes. Stir in the butter until melted. Taste and adjust the seasoning with more salt and pepper. Pour the sauce over the lamb and garnish with the parsley. Serve at once with the polenta.

6 lamb shanks (about 4½ pounds total)
Kosher salt and freshly ground black pepper
2 tablespoons extra-virgin olive oil
1 medium yellow onion, finely chopped
2 medium carrots, peeled and finely chopped
2 stalks celery, finely chopped
3 cloves garlic, minced
2 tablespoons tomato paste
1½ cups dry red wine
2 cups low-sodium beef stock
1 (15-ounce) can tomato sauce
2 sprigs fresh thyme
2 sprigs fresh oregano
2 tablespoons unsalted butter
Chopped fresh flat-leaf parsley, for garnish
Creamy Polenta (page 200), for serving (optional)

A LEG OF LAMB IS USUALLY considered a special-occasion cut, for holidays like Easter or Christmas (which of course it is great for), but our family loves to cook one any time of year. Like many larger cuts of meat, it may seem a bit intimidating if you've never cooked one before, but a leg of lamb is more approachable than you might think! The timeless combination of rosemary and garlic complement the earthy flavor of lamb and is so aromatic when roasting. Just remember the most important indicator of doneness is the internal temperature of the meat, so don't just rely on timing. For big roasts like this, I let it rest for at least fifteen minutes before carving to that the juices redistribute within the meat, leaving it deliciously moist.

# GARLIC–ROSEMARY ROASTED LEG OF LAMB

*Makes 6 to 8 servings*

Using a mortar and pestle or the flat side of a chef's knife, pound and smash the garlic and spice rub together into a paste. Transfer to a small bowl and stir in the olive oil, rosemary, and pepper.

If the lamb has a fatty side, score it in a crisscross pattern, cutting down only as far as the meat. Spread the paste all over the lamb and set aside at room temperature for 30 minutes, or cover and refrigerate up to overnight. (If refrigerated, let it sit at room temperature for 1 hour before cooking.)

Preheat the oven to 450 degrees F. Heat a cast-iron pan, large enough to hold the leg of lamb, over medium-high heat until hot. Place the lamb in the hot pan, then transfer immediately to the oven. Roast for 20 minutes, turning once halfway through. Turn the lamb once more, then reduce the temperature to 325 degrees F. Continue to roast until nicely browned and an instant-read thermometer inserted into the thickest part of the leg (away from the bone) registers 135 degrees F for medium-rare, 35 to 45 minutes longer, depending on its size.

Transfer the lamb to a cutting board, cover loosely with aluminum foil, and let rest for 15 to 20 minutes. Carve into thin slices and serve.

6 cloves garlic, minced
1 tablespoon M5 Spice Rub (page 127)
2 tablespoons extra-virgin olive oil
1 tablespoon minced fresh rosemary leaves
½ teaspoon freshly ground black pepper
1 (4- to 6-pound) semi-boneless leg of lamb

On the Side

**H**AVING A KITCHEN GARDEN BESIDE our house makes it easy to add freshly picked seasonal veggies to the dinner table. We grow most of the herbs I use (see page 205), and we harvest from the rhubarb patch and the Japanese plum, pear, and apple trees that grow at the guesthouse. We also forage all types of wild berries from the vines and bushes scattered around the ranch. This means the majority of our garden space is reserved for vegetables.

Our garden isn't made up of neat rows of raised beds. It's more of a lush, mostly fenced in, wild patch of green that we have to carefully wade through as we hunt for treasures. I've heard this method called "chaos gardening," but it's just the way our garden tends to grow!

We have a fairly short growing season since the ranch is at three thousand feet elevation and we can get a frost any day of the year. This keeps us mostly focused on what we can get in the ground and growing quickly as soon as the last big freeze is over in late spring and throughout the summer.

In the spring we put in lots of lettuce varieties so we have fresh salad greens, as well as potatoes, onions, eggplant, and sweet peas. Summer is our main growing season, and that's when the garden gets really abundant. Tomatoes, hot peppers, cucumbers, zucchini, squash, melons, pumpkins, and artichokes create a plentiful garden that you could almost get lost in. It's so much fun to jump into the greenery and see what we can unearth for dinner that night.

The girls love to help in the garden. Maisie is fond of artichokes, Francie prefers broccoli and brussels sprouts, Janie likes al dente asparagus, and Tess thinks cucumbers and zucchini are the best. Tess in particular likes to garden—she gives pet names to the veggies she plants and then checks on their progress as they grow. Last year she had a pumpkin vine she named Orange Juice that grew twenty feet long, and an eggplant that she called Grape Juice.

All of these vegetables, as well as the seasonal produce we buy at local farm stands, go into our favorite salads and side dishes. Simple and colorful, there's nothing better than a platter of roasted asparagus, a shaved zucchini salad, or a quick sauté of green beans, corn, and cherry tomatoes. We always have piles of potatoes in various guises to feed those hearty appetites! What follows are some of our tried-and-true favorites for serving alongside any main dish, or to enjoy on their own.

WE GROW MANY VARIETIES OF summer and winter squashes in our garden. I tend to plant more starts than I intend to and often end up with overflowing baskets of fresh vegetables in my kitchen and at Camp. They grow well at our elevation: one year Tess planted a tiny pumpkin vine, and it busted through the garden fence and stretched alongside the cabin with huge pumpkins dotting the vine. This tangy salad makes the most of a bounty and is particularly pretty if you use different colors and types of summer squashes (but avoid pattypan because they are difficult to peel into ribbons). The toasted pine nuts and salty cheese are lovely counterparts to the natural sweetness of the squash.

# SHAVED SUMMER SQUASH SALAD WITH TOASTED PINE NUTS

*Makes 6 servings*

In a small, dry skillet over medium-low heat, toast the pine nuts, shaking the pan occasionally, until lightly toasted, about 3 minutes. Remove from the heat and let cool.

Using a vegetable peeler, shave long strips of the squashes from end to end into a wide serving bowl. As you shave the ribbons, rotate the squash, shaving it down to the seed core. Discard the core.

Drizzle the squash ribbons with the olive oil, then squeeze the lemon over the top. Season with salt and pepper and toss to coat the ribbons evenly. Using the vegetable peeler, shave the cheese over the squash, then sprinkle with the pine nuts and basil. Serve at once.

¼ cup pine nuts

2½ pounds mixed zucchini and yellow squash

2 tablespoons extra-virgin olive oil

½ medium lemon

Kosher salt and freshly ground black pepper

1 ounce pecorino Romano, ricotta salata, Asiago, or Parmesan cheese

2 tablespoons chopped fresh basil or flat-leaf parsley leaves

ROASTED VEGGIES OF ALL SORTS are a big hit in our house. Cauliflower is a favorite because there are so many ways you can play with the flavor, and it goes with just about everything. Brian prefers this version because he loves anything with a little kick to it, like this spicy buffalo sauce. You can use the same roasting method for more than just cauliflower, though—broccoli and winter squash are equally terrific. If you aren't in the mood for buffalo sauce, experiment with other accompaniments: toss the roasted cauliflower with a splash of vinegar and dried currants, or lemon zest and chopped green olives.

# M5 ROASTED CAULIFLOWER <u>WITH</u> BUFFALO SAUCE

*Makes 6 servings*

Preheat the oven to 425 degrees F. Pile the cauliflower on a large rimmed baking sheet, drizzle with the olive oil, and toss until evenly coated. Season with the spice rub or with salt and pepper, and toss until evenly coated. Spread into a single layer. Roast, stirring once, until the cauliflower is tender and nicely caramelized on the edges, about 20 minutes.

While the cauliflower roasts, in a small saucepan over medium-low heat, warm the hot sauce and butter, stirring often, until the butter is melted. Pour into a small bowl.

Transfer the cauliflower to a shallow serving bowl. Serve the sauce alongside or drizzle it over the top. Garnish with celery leaves and serve warm.

1 (1½-pound) head cauliflower, cored and cut into florets
3 tablespoons extra-virgin olive oil
¾ teaspoon M5 Spice Rub (see page 127), or kosher salt and freshly ground black pepper
¼ cup hot sauce, such as Crystal or Frank's RedHot
2 tablespoons unsalted butter, cut into pieces
Celery leaves, for garnish (optional)

ON THE SIDE

WE MAKE COLESLAW FOR LOTS of our summer barbecues and gatherings—it is an ideal accompaniment to pulled pork sandwiches and ribs. Maisie is such a coleslaw fan that she taught herself how to make it, and now her sisters insist she whip up a batch whenever they smell pulled pork (page 141) simmering away in the slow cooker. This version, which has a great balance of vinegar and sweetness with the subtle flavor of celery seed, has good Southern roots. It was inspired by my sister, Baby Ann, who lives deep in the heart of Nashville.

# CREAMY COLESLAW

*Makes 8 servings*

Using a chef's knife, quarter and core the cabbage. Cut each wedge thinly into fine shreds and place in a large serving bowl. Using a box grater, shred the carrots on the large holes. Add it and the shallot to the bowl.

In a small bowl, whisk together the mayonnaise, sugar, lemon juice, vinegar, celery seeds, salt, and pepper. Pour over the cabbage and toss until well combined. Cover and refrigerate for at least 30 minutes and up to 4 hours before serving. The coleslaw will keep for up to 2 days in the refrigerator.

1 (1½- to 2-pound) head green
   cabbage
2 medium carrots, peeled
1 medium shallot, finely
   chopped
¾ cup mayonnaise
2 tablespoons sugar
Juice of ½ medium lemon
   (about 2 tablespoons)
2 tablespoons white wine vinegar
   or unseasoned rice vinegar
½ teaspoon celery seeds
¼ teaspoon kosher salt
¼ teaspoon freshly ground
   black pepper

THIS SALAD IS SO POPULAR at the Burgerhouse that we now serve it year-round. The crispy-brown, barely cooked sprouts and tangy-sweet citrus dressing are such a unique combination. It is a good way to get brussels sprout haters to change their minds—after only one bite! We add toasted almonds to the salad, but pecans or walnuts would be right at home in this dish too.

# CRISPY BRUSSELS SPROUT SALAD <u>WITH</u> CITRUS–MAPLE VINAIGRETTE

*Makes 6 servings*

To make the vinaigrette, add the orange juice, vinegar, maple syrup, lemon juice, and mustard to a blender and blend until well combined. With the blender running, slowly add the olive oil until the dressing is emulsified. Season with salt and pepper. You should have about 1 cup vinaigrette. Store in a jar for up to 1 week in the refrigerator.

To make the salad, in a large cast-iron skillet over medium-high heat, warm the oil until very hot but not smoking. Carefully add the sprouts to the pan, cut side down, and cook until crisp-tender and golden brown on the cut sides, about 4 minutes. Using a slotted spoon, transfer the sprouts to paper towels to drain and cool. Sprinkle with salt while still warm.

In a large wide serving bowl, toss together the lettuce, apple, and sprouts with about ¼ cup of the vinaigrette. Top with the almonds, cheese, and chives and serve at once, passing the remaining vinaigrette alongside.

**FOR THE VINAIGRETTE**
⅓ cup freshly squeezed orange juice (from about 2 oranges)
2 tablespoons apple cider vinegar
1 tablespoon maple syrup
1 tablespoon freshly squeezed lemon juice
1 teaspoon Dijon mustard
½ cup extra-virgin olive oil
Kosher salt and freshly ground black pepper

**FOR THE SALAD**
½ cup vegetable oil
1 pound small brussels sprouts, trimmed and halved (quartered if large)
Kosher salt
8 to 10 ounces mixed baby lettuces
1 tart-sweet apple, such as Honeycrisp or Pink Lady, quartered and thinly sliced crosswise
⅓ cup sliced or slivered almonds, toasted
2 to 3 ounces Asiago cheese, shaved
1 tablespoon packed chopped fresh chives

AS SOON AS ASPARAGUS IS in season in the springtime, I am always reminded to make this recipe. Roasted asparagus is one of my favorite vegetable dishes; I grew up with it as a staple in family dinners. You can serve it simply with a drizzle of olive oil and some salt and pepper, but the addition of fresh spring herbs and a tangy lemon vinaigrette with chopped hard-boiled eggs and briny capers really takes it to the next level. This is an elegant choice for sharing at a big brunch or lunch.

# ROASTED ASPARAGUS <u>WITH</u> EGG–CAPER VINAIGRETTE

*Makes 6 servings*

Fill a small bowl with ice and cold water to create an ice bath. Fill a small saucepan halfway with water and place over high heat. When the water boils, using a slotted spoon, gently add the eggs. Reduce the heat to medium and gently boil until the eggs are hard-cooked, about 12 minutes. Use the slotted spoon to transfer them to the ice bath.

Preheat the oven to 425 degrees F. In a bowl, whisk together the vinegar, shallot, mustard, ¼ teaspoon salt, and a few grinds of pepper. Let stand for 10 minutes, then whisk in the olive oil. Stir in the parsley and capers. Peel and dice the eggs and stir into the dressing.

Snap the woody ends off the asparagus. Spread the asparagus on a rimmed baking sheet in an even layer, drizzle with a little olive oil, and season with salt. Roast, stirring once halfway, until just crisp-tender, 5 to 7 minutes.

Transfer the asparagus to a serving plate and pour the dressing over the top. Serve warm or at room temperature.

2 large eggs
2 tablespoons sherry vinegar
1 tablespoon minced shallot
1 teaspoon Dijon mustard
Kosher salt and freshly ground black pepper
¼ cup extra-virgin olive oil
¼ cup finely chopped fresh flat-leaf parsley leaves, plus more torn leaves for garnish
1 tablespoon packed chopped capers
2 bunches (about 2 pounds) medium-thick asparagus

**THIS IS THE SALAD TO SERVE** anyone who claims they don't love kale, because it's too tough. The secret to tender kale is to massage it gently with a little salt and lemon zest before tossing in the rest of the ingredients. I love the balance of flavors and textures here too: salty Parmesan, crisp bacon, garlic-infused olive oil, and just enough balsamic to sweeten it up. And, unlike other salads, this one just gets better when it is made and dressed a little in advance. It's super the next day with a fried egg on top!

# CHOPPED KALE SALAD <u>WITH</u> PARMESAN, LEMON, BACON, AND BALSAMIC

*Makes 6 servings*

In a skillet over medium heat, fry the bacon until crisp, about 6 minutes. Transfer to paper towels to drain. Discard the bacon grease (or save for another use).

Reduce the heat to medium-low and add the olive oil and garlic (no need to wipe out the pan). Cook, stirring occasionally, until the garlic turns golden, about 3 minutes. Remove the pan from the heat and set aside to cool completely.

Strip the stems from the kale and discard. Wash the leaves, chop into bite-size pieces, and place in a large salad bowl. Sprinkle with the salt, then add the lemon zest and juice. Using your hands, massage the kale until it starts to look a little wilted, about 1 minute.

Using a fine-mesh sieve, drain the garlic oil into a small bowl. Discard the garlic (or save for another use). Add the reserved bacon, about two-thirds of the Parmesan, 1 tablespoon of the garlic oil, and 1 tablespoon balsamic to the kale. Toss until well coated. Taste and adjust the seasoning with more salt, balsamic, or oil. Garnish with the remaining Parmesan and serve.

4 thick-cut slices applewood-smoked bacon (about 6 ounces), chopped

2 tablespoons extra-virgin olive oil

3 cloves garlic, peeled and smashed

2 bunches (about 1 pound) lacinato (dinosaur) kale

¼ teaspoon kosher salt

Finely grated zest and juice of 1 small Meyer lemon (or ½ medium Eureka lemon)

¼ cup freshly grated Parmesan cheese

1 to 2 tablespoons balsamic vinegar

WHEN OUR SUMMER GARDEN IS abundant with fresh green beans and sweet cherry tomatoes, this is my go-to side dish. It's great with any grilled meat, plus it's quick and easy to throw together at the last minute, especially if you blanch the green beans in advance (sometimes I'll do it in the morning). If you are planting your own beans, it's fun to grow different varieties: green, wax, and even purple. Whichever herbs I have in the garden end up in this dish, so feel free to experiment with new combinations depending on what you have on hand.

# FRESH CORN, GREEN BEAN, AND CHERRY TOMATO SAUTÉ

*Makes 6 servings*

First, blanch the green beans. Fill a bowl with ice and cold water and set aside. Bring a medium saucepan filled halfway with salted water to a boil over high heat. Reduce the heat to medium and add the green beans. Cook until just crisp-tender, about 4 minutes (depending upon their size and freshness), then drain in a colander and transfer to the ice bath. Set aside.

To prepare the corn, snap the ears in half crosswise. Stand each one on the flat end and, using a sharp knife, cut down the side of the cob to remove the kernels.

In a deep skillet over medium-high heat, warm the oil. Add the corn, tomatoes, herbs, and a sprinkle of salt and pepper, and cook, stirring, until the corn is just barely tender, about 3 minutes.

Drain the green beans and add to the corn mixture. Cook, stirring, until the mixture is warmed through. Add the lemon juice and butter and stir to combine. Season with salt and pepper. Serve hot or at room temperature.

1 pound fresh green beans or a combination of green and wax beans, trimmed and halved crosswise

2 ears fresh white corn, shucked

1 tablespoon extra-virgin olive oil

2 cups halved sweet cherry tomatoes (about 12 ounces)

2 teaspoons finely chopped mixed fresh herbs, such as oregano, marjoram, thyme, and basil

Kosher salt and freshly ground black pepper

Juice of ½ medium lemon (about 2 tablespoons)

2 tablespoons unsalted butter

CREAMY AND BUTTERY, HAND-STIRRED POLENTA is a side I make frequently both for our retreats and for cozy dinners at home. Guests who have been at the retreats always ask me about it wistfully afterward, so I'm thrilled to be able to share this recipe. Start with good-quality corn grits or polenta. Sometimes I use milk, but swapping it for buttermilk gives the polenta an amazing tangy flavor. I love serving it with braised meats like short ribs (page 114) or lamb shanks (page 178), and the leftovers are excellent warmed in a saucepan with a little milk or buttermilk to bring back that smooth silky consistency, even after it's been in the fridge a day or two.

# CREAMY PARMESAN POLENTA

*Makes 6 to 8 servings*

In a large heavy saucepan or Dutch oven over medium heat, melt 4 tablespoons of the butter. Add the onion and a sprinkle of salt and cook, stirring occasionally, until softened but not browned, about 5 minutes. Increase the heat to medium-high and add the milk, water, and 1 teaspoon salt. Bring to a boil, then slowly pour the polenta into the pan while whisking constantly. Cook, still whisking constantly, for 2 minutes, then reduce the heat to low and cover the pan.

Simmer, stirring well with a wooden spoon every 10 minutes, until the polenta is thick and creamy, about 45 minutes total.

Remove from the heat and stir in the remaining 4 tablespoons butter until melted. Add the cheese and stir to combine. If the polenta is too thick, add milk until it reaches the desired consistency. Taste and season with salt and pepper as needed. Serve at once.

8 tablespoons unsalted butter, divided

1 small yellow onion, finely chopped

Kosher salt and freshly ground black pepper

2 cups whole milk or well-shaken buttermilk

4 cups water or low-sodium beef or vegetable broth

1½ cups polenta (corn grits)

½ cup freshly grated Parmesan or aged or smoked cheddar cheese

THIS CAST-IRON POTATO DISH MAKES an impressive presentation (it always gets rave reviews on Instagram!), but it's nearly effortless to put together. The secret is to place chopsticks or thin wooden spoon handles on either side of the potatoes so when you cut into them, the knife doesn't go all the way through. I like these on the simpler side, seasoned with M5 Spice Rub and baked with plenty of butter. We usually serve them with sour cream, but you can load them up with crisp bacon and shredded cheese just before they come out of the oven (just give it a few minutes to let the cheese melt).

# CAST-IRON HASSELBACK POTATOES

*Makes 6 servings*

Preheat the oven to 425 degrees F. Grease a 12-inch cast-iron pan with butter or bacon fat.

Cut each potato crosswise into ⅛-inch-thick slices without cutting all the way through to the bottom—leave about ¼ inch of the potato intact (this will help hold them together). A good trick is to lay two chopsticks on either side of the potato to keep the knife from going all the way through. Arrange the potatoes in the pan with about an inch in between.

Brush the potatoes all over with half of the butter. Sprinkle evenly with 1 teaspoon of the spice rub. Cover the pan with aluminum foil and bake for 30 minutes.

Remove the foil and drizzle the potatoes, which should have opened up slightly, with the remaining butter and the remaining 1 teaspoon spice rub. Bake uncovered until the potatoes are crispy on the edges and soft in the center, about 15 minutes longer. Garnish with the parsley, then serve with sour cream.

5 tablespoons unsalted butter, melted, divided, plus more for greasing the pan

6 medium russet or Yukon Gold potatoes (about 1½ pounds total)

2 teaspoons M5 Spice Rub (see page 127), divided

2 tablespoons chopped fresh flat-leaf parsley leaves, for garnish

Sour cream, for serving

ON THE SIDE

201

**THE GIRLS AND I ARE** pretty sure this is the most fun way to make potatoes. If you've been stuck in a roasted or baked potato rut, try this fresh take. It's also great for getting the kids involved in dinner prep: I hand out mason jars and let the girls smash away. The drizzle of herb butter before roasting is my favorite part because it infuses the potatoes with flavor. The end result is somewhere between baked potatoes and mashed potatoes, and their rustic texture pairs beautifully with steak or other protein. Sprinkling them with some M5 Spice Rub (see page 127) is also a good idea!

# HERB-ROASTED SMASHER POTATOES

*Makes 6 servings*

Preheat the oven to 450 degrees F. Add the potatoes to a large saucepan and fill with enough water just to cover them. Add 2 tablespoons salt. Bring to a boil over high heat, then reduce the heat to medium-high and simmer until the potatoes are tender, 20 to 25 minutes. Drain in a colander and set aside.

Melt the butter in the same saucepan over medium heat. Add the garlic, herbs, 1 teaspoon salt, and ¼ teaspoon pepper. Stir until fragrant, about 1 minute. Add the potatoes and gently toss to coat.

Using a slotted spoon, transfer the potatoes to a large rimmed baking sheet and spread into an even layer. Using the bottom of a flat drinking glass or a mason jar, gently smash each potato until it splits and is about ½ to ¾ inch thick. Scrape any remaining herb butter from the pan over the potatoes.

Roast the potatoes, without turning, until crisp and golden brown on the bottom, about 20 minutes. Serve at once.

2 to 2½ pounds small whole (unpeeled) Yukon Gold potatoes
Kosher salt and freshly ground black pepper
6 tablespoons unsalted butter
3 cloves garlic, minced
2 tablespoons packed finely chopped mixed herbs, such as oregano, rosemary, thyme, and parsley

# A KITCHEN HERB GARDEN

We are lucky enough to have lots of space near our cabin to grow vegetables, fruits, and herbs. You don't need a lot of property, though—an herb garden can be grown in pretty much any amount of space, whether you have a raised bed in your backyard or just a few small pots on a windowsill. Herbs are super easy to grow and require little maintenance, so they can be a fun way to get kids involved in gardening too. Another benefit of an herb garden is that you always have access to a fresh sprig or two, which can brighten up nearly any savory meal or cocktail.

Flat-leaf parsley, basil, thyme, rosemary, oregano, and lavender are all staples in our kitchen. I also like to grow a few varieties of mint and sage. Start by planting whatever you like to use most frequently in your cooking—basil for caprese salads, sage to mix into butter and put atop steak, fistfuls of parsley for chimichurri sauce—and then branch out from there. The girls like trying unique herbs like chocolate mint, lemon thyme, or striped variegated sage. Note that mint should be planted in its own container since the roots can take over, but everything else can be grown together. Marigolds are also a great addition to any garden to add a little color and help repel insects.

SWEET POTATOES ARE A BIG favorite of Brian's—and so is ranch dressing—and in our house the two go hand in hand. It may seem like work to make ranch dressing yourself, but this version just needs a quick spin in the blender, so it's well worth the minimal effort. Try it on salads or avocado toast, drizzled over fresh sliced tomatoes, or use it as a sandwich spread. You won't want to go back to store-bought ranch after you've made your own!

# ROASTED SWEET POTATO FRIES <u>WITH</u> RANCH DRESSING

*Makes 6 servings*

To make the ranch, add the buttermilk, herbs, garlic powder, and onion powder to a blender. Pulse until well combined. Pour into a bowl, then whisk in the mayonnaise until smooth. Season to taste with salt, hot sauce, and/or lemon juice. You should have about 1½ cups. Cover and refrigerate until ready to use. The dressing can be stored in the refrigerator for up to 1 week.

To make the fries, position two oven racks evenly in the middle and upper third of the oven and preheat to 425 degrees F.

Trim the ends of the potatoes, then cut them lengthwise into ½-inch-thick slabs. Stack the slabs and cut lengthwise into ½-inch-wide batons. Transfer to a large wide bowl. Toss the potatoes first with the cornstarch to coat evenly, then drizzle with the oil and toss again to coat evenly. Divide the potatoes among two large rimmed baking sheets and arrange them in a single layer with space between.

Bake until the bottoms are golden, rotating the pans halfway through, about 13 minutes. Turn the potatoes and rotate them on the pan so they cook evenly, then continue to cook until the other side is golden brown, again rotating the pans halfway through, about 10 minutes longer. The fries should be tender on the inside and deeply golden on the outside. Season with salt and pepper. You can turn off the oven and leave the fries inside for up to 10 minutes to keep warm.

Transfer to a serving platter and serve hot, with the ranch dressing alongside for dipping.

**FOR THE DRESSING**
½ cup well-shaken buttermilk
1 teaspoon packed chopped
  fresh chives
1 teaspoon packed chopped
  fresh flat-leaf parsley
1 teaspoon packed chopped
  fresh dill
¼ teaspoon garlic powder
¼ teaspoon onion powder
1 cup mayonnaise
Kosher salt (optional)
Louisiana-style hot sauce
  (optional)
Freshly squeezed lemon juice
  (optional)

**FOR THE FRIES**
2 pounds orange sweet
  potatoes, peeled or unpeeled
2 tablespoons cornstarch,
  potato starch, or tapioca
  starch
2 tablespoons extra-virgin
  olive oil
Kosher salt and freshly ground
  black pepper

BAKED BEANS AND RANCH LIFE are the best combo. These rustic beans may take their sweet time to cook, but it's mostly hands-off time in the slow cooker. I prep the beans in the morning before heading out to take care of ranch chores—by the time I return, they are ready to eat! Exploding with sweet, tangy flavor, they go perfectly with pork ribs or pulled pork. I think they are best made with not-too-sweet sauce, such as my homemade Ranch-Barbecue Sauce (page 147). I love to use great-quality heirloom beans from a farm like Llano Seco, but you can use any kind of creamy beans you love. Sometimes I'll just have a bowlful topped with sliced avocado, jalapeños, and a dollop of sour cream, and that's dinner! They make great leftovers for lunch the next day too.

# RUSTIC BAKED BEANS

*Makes 8 servings*

Put the beans in a large bowl and add enough cold water to cover by about 2 inches; let soak overnight. The next day, drain and rinse the beans.

Add the beans and 8 cups water to a large pot. Bring to a boil over high heat, then reduce the heat to medium-high and gently boil the beans until just tender, which can take anywhere from 30 to 75 minutes depending on the age and type of bean.

While the beans cook, in a skillet over medium heat, cook the bacon, stirring, until it is crisp and the fat has rendered, about 6 minutes. Using a slotted spoon, transfer the bacon to paper towels to drain. Pour off all but 2 tablespoons of the fat in the pan. Add the onion and a sprinkle of salt and cook, stirring, until the onion softens and starts to brown, about 5 minutes. Add the jalapeño and garlic and cook, stirring, until fragrant, about 1 minute.

Add the stock, barbecue sauce, ketchup, brown sugar, molasses, mustard, vinegar, hot sauce, and ½ teaspoon black pepper to the skillet and stir to combine. Bring to a boil over medium-high heat. Stir in the reserved bacon, then set aside until the beans are ready.

When the beans are ready, drain them in a colander and place in a 6- to 8-quart slow cooker. Pour the sauce over the beans. Cover and cook on high for 4 hours or low for 6 hours. Let sit for about 15 minutes before serving. The beans will thicken as they cool.

1 pound small dried beans, such as great northern or navy

4 thick-cut slices bacon (about 6 ounces), chopped

1 small yellow onion, finely chopped

Kosher salt and freshly ground black pepper

1 small jalapeño, seeded and minced

3 cloves garlic, minced

1½ cups low-sodium chicken stock

1 cup barbecue sauce, homemade (page 147) or store-bought

½ cup ketchup

¼ cup packed dark brown sugar

1 tablespoon dark molasses (not blackstrap)

1 tablespoon brown mustard

1 tablespoon apple cider vinegar

1 tablespoon hot sauce

BRIAN DECLARED THIS THE "BEST cornbread I've ever tasted," and everyone always comments on its silkiness. It's not your average cornbread! Baking and serving it in a cast-iron skillet makes it look great on the table, but you can also use a baking dish. Serve it with a big scoop of honey butter (which is equally delicious spread on our homemade English muffins, page 33) and enjoy every savory bite.

# SKILLET CORNBREAD
## WITH HONEY BUTTER

*Makes 6 to 8 servings*

To make the honey butter, in a small bowl, use a fork to smash and stir together the butter, honey, and salt until well combined. Cover and refrigerate for at least 30 minutes before using.

Preheat the oven to 425 degrees F. Grease a 10-inch cast-iron skillet or 8-inch square baking dish.

To make the cornbread, in a large bowl, whisk together the cornmeal, flour, sugar, baking powder, and salt. In a small bowl, whisk together the milk, eggs, and butter. Add the wet ingredients to the dry ingredients and stir until just combined. Scrape the batter into the prepared pan.

Bake until the top is lightly golden and a toothpick inserted into the center comes out clean, about 17 minutes. Let cool for 10 minutes before serving with the honey butter.

**FOR THE HONEY BUTTER**
½ cup (1 stick) unsalted butter, at room temperature
2 tablespoons good-quality honey
¼ teaspoon kosher salt

**FOR THE CORNBREAD**
1 cup fine cornmeal
1 cup all-purpose flour
¼ cup sugar
1 tablespoon baking powder
1 teaspoon kosher salt
1 cup whole milk
2 large eggs
6 tablespoons unsalted butter, melted

Five O' Clock
Cocktails

**A**T THE END OF A LONG day on the ranch, there's nothing better than a five o'clock cocktail with Brian. Sometimes we'll grab an ice-cold "chore beer" to make the evening rounds. When we finally call it a day, I'll juice some citrus and add bourbon, then shake it in a cocktail shaker and pour my favorite drink. Only then do I kick my boots off and feel like I earned it. Our evening ritual extends to family and friends or whoever might be visiting. Most know that they'll be offered a sidecar or a chore beer shortly after arrival if it's late afternoon.

So it was no surprise that we jumped at an opportunity to purchase and rehabilitate the historic bar in downtown Fort Jones in 2017. The old stone building had continuously been a bar since the 1850s and came with the original post-prohibition liquor license. It also has a secret prohibition basement, with the original call bell used to warn patrons in those days. We wanted to continue that tradition and create an inviting space to share our ranch-raised meats and private label whiskey and bourbons with everyone. The bar needed a lot of work, but it had good bones. We rebuilt a beautiful multitextured backdrop behind the existing sugar pine bartop (a massive piece of wood that took thirty men to carry across the highway and install!). The building has the original tin ceiling and old wood floors, but has updated amenities like a full commercial kitchen and a new back deck and yard for games and live music.

It has become a hub of the community, filled with locals and tourists who come from all over the world. Our bar stocks over a hundred varieties of whiskey and bourbon, including our own Five Marys label. Our sidecars—my favorite!—are served five ways, plus we offer signature cocktails like spicy jalapeño margaritas, a great Bloody Mary, and our ranch mimosas topped with a splash of gin. We also create a cocktail of the week that allows us to use whatever seasonal bounty we have growing in the garden at that time. We kick off every Friday night with live music from local bands; it's our most popular night of the week and feels like we are opening our living room to the entire town.

THIS DRINK HAS BECOME SO well known at the Burgerhouse bar that people come from all over to sample it. Traditionally sidecars are made with brandy, but I'm a bourbon lover, so I had to adapt it accordingly. We always try to use Meyer lemons, which are more fragrant and sweeter than regular lemons, and I recommend using them if you can. If you want your cocktail a little less boozy, substitute maple syrup or honey simple syrup (page 226) for the orange liqueur. At the bar, we sometimes use jalapeño simple syrup (page 226) for a kicked-up version, or alternatively, top it with seltzer to lighten it up.

# MARY'S LEMON– BOURBON SIDECARS

*Makes 2 cocktails*

Pour the sugar into a shallow dish. Rub the rims of two sidecar glasses with the lemon wedge and dip the rims in the sugar to create a sugared rim.

Fill a cocktail shaker half full with ice. Add the lemon juice, bourbon, and orange liqueur. Cover and shake. Strain into the prepared glasses and serve.

2 tablespoons sugar
1 Meyer lemon wedge
Ice, cubed or crushed
½ cup freshly squeezed Meyer lemon juice (from about 3 Meyer lemons)
½ cup (4 ounces) bourbon
¼ cup (2 ounces) orange liqueur, preferably Cointreau, or maple syrup or honey simple syrup

MAKING COCKTAILS FOR A CROWD is always easier when you can do it in a pitcher. It gives you some time to relax with your guests between batches, instead of playing bartender. Whiskey punch feels old-fashioned (in a good way, because . . . whiskey!), so I like to pour it from a cute vintage pitcher into a bunch of pretty, mismatched vintage glasses. It makes it so fun to serve to guests, and it fits the theme. This recipe is just a starting point and can easily be adjusted according to your tastes, like substituting a different juice or using lemon-lime soda instead of ginger ale. Whiskey is a great option because it gives it a nice deep flavor, but I recommend using a sweet (not smoky) one for a crowd-pleasing punch.

# WHISKEY PUNCH

*Makes 1 pitcher*

Fill a large pitcher half full with ice. Pour the ingredients into the pitcher in the following order: first the cranberry juice, then lemon juice, then whiskey, and finally ginger ale. Do not stir. Add lemon slices to the rim of the pitcher. Stir just before serving within 30 minutes.

Ice cubes
4 cups cranberry juice
¼ cup freshly squeezed lemon juice (from about 1 lemon)
2 cups sweet whiskey or bourbon
4 cups ginger ale
Lemon slices

## FIVE MARYS BOURBON

When we moved to the ranch, I became a bourbon girl. It started with a sidecar cocktail, which traditionally has brandy, that I modified to my taste, swapping in bourbon and using sweeter Meyer lemons. About three years ago, we decided to partner with our friends Steve and Amy Bohner, who had started a craft distillery called Alchemy Distillery in Arcata, which is on the California coast. They loved that our mission at Five Marys was in line with theirs: making small batches, sourcing the best ingredients, and being passionate about the product we are making. It felt like a natural partnership. Our bourbon (a type of whiskey that is made with at least 51 percent corn) and whiskey are made with grains sourced from local farmers. Every step, from aging the barrels to carefully honing the flavor profile, is carefully thought out so that the end result is smooth and rich, perfect for sipping or using in a cocktail. We've won awards and accolades in the whiskey world, but the biggest compliment to us and our distillers is the feedback from guests that it's the best darn whiskey and bourbon they've ever tried!

SUNDAYS ARE A DAY WE TRY to take life a little slower. It's usually a family day, but sometimes we enjoy having friends over for brunch after church. In that case, it calls for some really good Bloody Marys for the adults. We like them extra spicy, but this recipe is so flexible you can tailor it to whatever tastes best to you. Just start with good ingredients and you can't go wrong. My favorite garnishes are pickled veggies—I grow a ton of green beans, which we pickle for use at the Burgerhouse and at home too. Pickled asparagus, carrot spears, and cauliflower are also fun additions to a Bloody Mary.

# SPICY BLOODY MARYS

*Makes 2 to 4 cocktails*

Pour the salt and chili powder into a shallow dish and stir to combine. Rub the rims of two pint glasses or four highball glasses with the lime wedge and dip the glasses in the mixture to create a salted rim.

In a small pitcher or container, whisk together the tomato juice, citrus juices, horseradish, Worcestershire, pickle juice, pepperoncini juice, celery salt, hot sauce, and a few grinds of pepper. Fill the glasses about three-quarters full of ice and add 1½ to 3 ounces vodka to each glass. Divide the tomato mixture among the glasses.

For each glass, spear 1 onion, 1 green olive, and 1 pepperoncini onto a toothpick. Place one across the rim of each glass, then garnish with a lime wedge and 3 dilly beans.

2 tablespoons kosher salt

1 teaspoon chili powder

1 lime wedge

2 cups (16 ounces) tomato juice

3 tablespoons freshly squeezed lemon juice

1 tablespoon freshly squeezed lime juice

1 tablespoon prepared horseradish (not horseradish sauce)

2 teaspoons Worcestershire sauce

2 teaspoons dill pickle juice, or 1 teaspoon olive brine

1 teaspoon pepperoncini juice (optional)

⅛ teaspoon celery salt

A few shakes hot sauce

Freshly ground black pepper

Ice

¾ cup (6 ounces) vodka

**FOR GARNISH**

2 to 4 pickled cocktail onions

2 to 4 pitted green olives

2 to 4 pepperoncini

2 to 4 lime wedges

6 to 12 dilly beans

## DIXIE AND ME

My number one sidekick is a sweet little dog named Dixie. She is a mutt, but from what we can guess, she's part Jack Russell and part Yorkshire terrier with a little something extra probably mixed in there. She is never far from my side, always watchful, and is in the truck or quad—riding shotgun—as soon as she knows I'm heading for it. We got her right after we bought the ranch when she was a tiny rescue puppy. Dixie and I bonded during the many long hours driving back and forth to the Bay Area when Brian and I were relocating our family up to the ranch for good.

Dixie is as loyal as can be. She's smart and obedient mixed with anxious and nervous, but she makes it very clear to anyone around that I am her person. She loves when I cook and lies down next to my feet, hoping for a taste of whatever meat I might be making. She sleeps on one of our sheep pelts in a little wire basket under my desk when I'm working at the Farm Store and stays cozy in my sock drawer in our bedroom closet at night. Dixie is one of a kind, and I'm lucky to have such a loyal

MY SISTER-IN-LAW KATHERINE, who also happens to be one of my best friends, married a fifth-generation cattle rancher and now works the cattle up in Burns, Oregon. She and I love that we have this lifestyle in common. Like me, she cooks up big meals for events on their ranch, such as brandings, where there are lots of mouths to feed. We are both often in charge of family gatherings and the twice-annual cousin campout, so when we are planning activities for nineteen Heffernan cousins, we like to make a big batch of mimosas for the adults. This ranch-style version with a dash of gin really takes it to a whole new level.

# RANCH 75 MIMOSAS

*Makes 2 servings*

Divide the orange juice among two chilled champagne glasses, then top evenly with the sparkling wine. Pour ½ ounce gin into each glass, then top with a splash of grenadine. Garnish with half an orange slice.

½ cup freshly squeezed orange juice (from about 2 oranges)
½ cup sparkling wine or prosecco
1 ounce gin
Grenadine
1 slice orange, halved

MY GREAT-AUNT RUTH ALWAYS MADE this frothy, light eggnog for my mom's family holidays, and I took over the tradition long before I could even drink it. Every Christmas, my mom would host big extended-family gatherings, and while she was busy cooking, she put me to work—starting around age twelve—making this eggnog. It's still a hit when I make it every year. I'm glad I get to enjoy it now too!

# GREAT-AUNT RUTH'S EGGNOG

*Makes 6 servings (about 1½ quarts)*

In the bowl of a stand mixer fitted with the whisk attachment (or using a handheld mixer), beat the egg yolks until pale in color. With the mixer on, slowly add the sugar, beating until dissolved and the yolks are thick and very pale, about 5 minutes. Scrape down the sides of the bowl a few times with a silicone spatula. Remove the bowl from the mixer and, using a whisk, whisk in the brandy and rum, then whisk in the milk and cream until the mixture is well combined.

In a clean mixer bowl, beat the egg whites with a clean whisk attachment until medium peaks form. Do not overbeat. Using the whisk or a spatula, gently fold the egg whites into the cream mixture until well combined and fluffy. Divide evenly among six tumbler glasses and garnish with nutmeg.

3 large eggs, separated
⅓ cup sugar
¾ cup brandy
¼ cup dark Jamaican rum
1½ cups whole milk
1½ cups heavy cream
Freshly grated nutmeg, for garnish

THIS SPICY SPIN ON A classic margarita is a Camp favorite. We often shake them up alongside a big platter of steak nachos (page 69), or pair them with jalapeño poppers (page 57) for twice the kick. I grow jalapeños in my garden and believe there is no better way to use them fresh in a cocktail than this. I like mine extra spicy with a coarse salt rim, but you can adjust the amount of spiciness to your liking by using less jalapeño or removing the seeds.

# JALAPEÑO-LIME MARGARITAS

*Makes 2 servings*

Pour the salt into a shallow dish. Rub the rims of two glasses with 1 of the lime wedges and dip the rims in the salt to create a salted rim.

In a cocktail shaker, add the simple syrup and 4 of the jalapeño slices. Using a muddler, muddle the jalapeño until softened but still intact. Fill the shaker half full with ice. Add the tequila and lime juice and shake until well mixed. Divide evenly among the glasses. Garnish each glass with a lime wedge and jalapeño slice.

2 tablespoons kosher salt

3 lime wedges, divided

¼ cup honey simple syrup (see sidebar)

6 thick slices fresh jalapeño, divided

Ice

½ cup (4 ounces) tequila

½ cup freshly squeezed lime juice (from about 4 limes)

---

## SIMPLE SYRUP

Simple syrup is a great way to not only add sweetness to a cocktail but also flavor. It can be as straightforward as one part water to one part sugar, but it's also easy to infuse fresh herbs, spices, or other seasonings. Here are two of my favorites that we use at the Burgerhouse:

To make honey simple syrup, in a small saucepan over medium-low heat, warm ¼ cup honey with ¼ cup water, stirring until the honey dissolves. Let cool to room temperature, then transfer to an airtight container. The simple syrup will keep in the refrigerator for up to 2 weeks. (Makes about ½ cup.)

To make jalapeño simple syrup, in a small saucepan over medium-low heat, warm ¼ cup granulated sugar with ¼ cup water and a few slices of fresh jalapeño (depending on how spicy you like it), stirring until the sugar dissolves. Let cool to room temperature, then strain into an airtight container. It will keep in the refrigerator for up to 2 weeks. (Makes about ½ cup.)

Something
Sweet

**M**ANY OF THE RECIPES WE MAKE at home have been passed down from both sides of our families, especially when it comes to these desserts. When I was in high school, I made my first spiral-bound recipe book of all our family favorites and gave it to every relative so we wouldn't lose those great dishes. I was very close to my grandfather Jim Arnerich (my mom's father), and before he passed away I promised him I would keep the family traditions and his mother's recipes alive (even his favorite ravioli recipe that calls for cow brains!).

Using seasonal ingredients in desserts, especially if we can get them straight from the farm, comes to us naturally: my great-grandfather was a berry farmer in Watsonville, and Brian was raised on a farm where his father grew prunes, almonds, and walnuts. Brian and I both come from big families where hard work is revered and getting together is always cause for celebration—and a great excuse to prepare fantastic meals. We learned at an early age that the best ones start with great-quality ingredients and end with a delicious dessert.

We've passed these traditions on to the girls and we all like to bake together, but Francie is the dessert-maker of the house. She loves to bake banana-chocolate cake, my mom's apple crisp, or sweet drop biscuits served with fruit and cream. And she's pretty great at it! Maisie also enjoys helping, but she leans toward more savory baked goods, like our Camp favorites: English muffins and flaky buttermilk biscuits. The recipes in this chapter are some of our most treasured or cherished, hearty and sweet, from our family to yours.

GRILLED PEACHES IN SUMMER BRING back happy memories of when Brian and I first got married. We used to make them often, with a scoop of vanilla ice cream or a dollop of freshly whipped cream on top. Nowadays Francie happily whips together these fluffy, tender drop biscuits to serve with grilled peaches. The char from the grill brings out the flavor of summer stone fruits, so this method works well with not only peaches but nectarines and plums as well, or a mixture of whatever is ripe and ready.

# SWEET DROP BISCUITS <u>WITH</u> GRILLED PEACHES AND CREAM

*Makes 6 servings*

To make the biscuits, preheat the oven to 425 degrees F. Line a large rimmed baking sheet with parchment paper. In a large bowl, whisk together the flour, sugar, baking powder, and salt. In another bowl, whisk together the cream, butter, egg, and vanilla. Pour the wet ingredients into the dry ingredients and gently mix with a fork just until the mixture comes together into a soft dough (do not overmix or your biscuits will be tough).

Using two large spoons, drop 6 equal dollops of dough onto the prepared baking sheet, spacing them an inch or two apart. Bake until puffed and golden brown, about 18 minutes. Transfer to a wire rack to cool while you prepare the peaches and cream.

Prepare a grill for direct cooking over medium heat (about 400 degrees F) or heat a stovetop cast-iron grill pan. Place the peaches on a baking sheet. Lightly brush them all over with a little oil. Grill the peaches, cut side down, until tender but not mushy and nicely grill-marked, turning a few times, 6 to 9 minutes depending on the firmness of the peaches. Transfer to a cutting board.

When cool enough to handle, thinly slice the peaches and transfer to a shallow mixing bowl. Sprinkle the sugar over them, and gently stir to combine. Set aside.

To make the whipped cream, add the cream, sugar, and vanilla to a mixing bowl. Using a whisk or electric mixer, beat until soft peaks form. Do not overbeat.

To assemble, place each biscuit on a dessert plate, then split them horizontally. Divide the peaches with juices among the bottom halves of the biscuits, scoop a big dollop of whipped cream over, and top with the other half of each biscuit.

**FOR THE BISCUITS**

2 cups all-purpose flour

¼ cup sugar

2 teaspoons baking powder

½ teaspoon kosher salt

1¼ cups heavy cream

6 tablespoons unsalted butter, melted

1 large egg

1 teaspoon vanilla extract

**FOR THE PEACHES**

6 ripe but slightly firm peaches, halved

Canola oil

About ¼ cup sugar (depending on sweetness of peaches)

**FOR THE WHIPPED CREAM**

1½ cups heavy cream

2 tablespoons sugar

1 teaspoon vanilla extract

**BRIAN AND I LOVE CHEESECAKE.** For our first anniversary I had a cheesecake delivered to our hotel in Hawaii where we were celebrating! But this cheesecake is a style all its own and quickly became our favorite way to enjoy the decadent dessert. Tart-sweet rhubarb puree gives the cheesecake a delicate pink hue, and the blackberry compote on top adds a perfect pop of flavor. The pistachio crust contributes richness and just the right amount of savory balance. This more rustic version of a cheesecake is as beautiful as it is delicious, and the unique presentation is definitely worth the extra effort for a special occasion.

# RHUBARB CHEESECAKE WITH PISTACHIO CRUST AND BLACKBERRY COMPOTE

*Makes 6 to 8 servings*

To make the rhubarb puree, in a medium saucepan over medium heat, stir together the rhubarb, sugar, lemon juice, and water. Bring to a boil, reduce heat to medium-low, cover, and simmer until the rhubarb is very tender, about 7 minutes. Transfer the mixture to a food processor and process to a smooth puree. You should have about ½ cup puree. Set aside to cool completely.

To make the crust, preheat the oven to 350 degrees F. Grease a 9-inch springform pan with butter or cooking spray. In the clean bowl of the food processor, process the pistachios and almonds until finely ground. Add the graham crackers and process until finely ground. Add the butter, sugar, and salt and pulse until the mixture is well mixed and holds together when pressed in your hand.

Dump the crust mixture into the prepared pan and press it into an even layer across the bottom and about 1 inch up the sides. Bake until fragrant and toasted, about 10 minutes. Set aside to cool on a wire rack. (If the crust slumps or cracks during baking, just use the bottom of a glass to press it back into place while the crust is slightly warm.)

**FOR THE RHUBARB PUREE**
6 ounces (about 2 small stalks) trimmed rhubarb, diced
¼ cup sugar
1 tablespoon freshly squeezed lemon juice
1 tablespoon water

**FOR THE CRUST**
⅓ cup roasted pistachios
⅓ cup slivered almonds
7 graham crackers (3½ ounces)
¼ cup unsalted butter, melted, plus more for greasing the pan
2 tablespoons sugar
¼ teaspoon kosher salt

Reduce the oven temperature to 325 degrees F. In the clean bowl of the food processor, process the cream cheese, sugar, and salt until smooth. Add the reserved rhubarb puree, sour cream, and vanilla and process to combine. Scrape down the sides of the bowl with a silicone spatula. Add the eggs and egg yolk and process until well combined. Scrape down the sides of the bowl again, pulse again, then scrape the mixture into the crust.

Bake until the center is barely wobbly, about 35 minutes. Transfer to a wire rack to cool completely, then refrigerate until chilled and set, at least 4 hours or overnight.

When ready to serve, remove the cheesecake from the refrigerator and remove the sides of the pan. In a bowl, stir together the black-berries, sugar, and lemon juice with a fork, mashing the blackberries slightly to release their juices. Let sit for 10 minutes. Spoon the blackberries over the top of the cheesecake and serve.

**FOR THE CHEESECAKE**
1 pound cream cheese, at room
    temperature
½ cup sugar
¼ teaspoon kosher salt
½ cup sour cream
1 teaspoon vanilla extract
2 large whole eggs
1 large egg yolk

**FOR THE BLACKBERRY COMPOTE**
2 cups fresh blackberries,
    halved if large
¼ cup sugar
2 teaspoons freshly squeezed
    lemon juice

MAKING ICE CREAM IS ALWAYS a worthwhile pastime on summer days at Camp. This recipe is great because the base is a silky vanilla custard you can flavor any way you like. When berries are in season, we puree them and make the prettiest purple ice cream. We use whatever berries we can find at our neighbor's u-pick patch or the wild blackberries that grow around the ranch (see page 241). You can make this in either a hand-crank or electric ice cream maker; just make sure it has at least a two-quart capacity so the ice cream doesn't overflow. Serve with additional fresh berries and plenty of whipped cream (Tess's favorite) on top.

# VERY BERRY ICE CREAM

*Makes about 1½ quarts*

Add the berries to a blender and blend to a smooth puree. Strain through a fine-mesh sieve into a bowl, pressing firmly on the puree with a silicone spatula; discard the seeds. You should have about 1½ cups puree. Refrigerate until ready to use.

Fill a large bowl with ice and cold water and nestle a second bowl in the ice bath. In a large saucepan over medium heat, whisk together the cream, milk, and ⅓ cup of the sugar, stirring gently until the mixture is steaming and the sugar dissolves. Remove from the heat. In a separate bowl, whisk the egg yolks with the remaining ⅓ cup sugar and the salt.

Add about ½ cup of the warm cream to the egg yolks, whisking as you add it, then whisk the egg yolk mixture into the saucepan as you add it. Return to medium-low or low heat, and simmer, stirring constantly, until the mixture thickens slightly and coats the back of a spoon, about 10 minutes. (Reduce the heat if it threatens to boil; do not let the mixture boil.)

Strain the custard through a fine-mesh sieve into the bowl set in the ice bath. Stir in the vanilla. Set aside until well chilled. (You can transfer to an airtight container and chill overnight.)

Stir the berry puree into the chilled custard. Transfer the mixture to an ice cream maker and process according to the manufacturer's instructions. Scrape the ice cream into an airtight container, press a piece of plastic wrap directly onto the ice cream, and freeze until solid (about 4 hours). Serve big scoops to a happy crowd!

2½ cups mixed fresh berries (about 14 ounces total), such as raspberries, blackberries, strawberries, and blueberries
2 cups heavy cream
1 cup whole milk
⅔ cup sugar, divided
6 large egg yolks
Pinch of kosher salt
1 teaspoon vanilla extract

# WILD BERRIES, WILD KIDS

Wild berries grow abundantly in our valley. During the hot summer months, blackberries and raspberries are bountiful, and you can find blueberries and even elderberries if you know where to look. I often send the girls out with pails to pick them. It doesn't take much encouragement to get them out there, but they usually come back with full bellies, stained fingers, and only a modest haul of berries! Their favorite place to pick is down by the river, where they ultimately get distracted and start catching frogs. The beautiful Scott River runs along the property line of our ranch, and it's one of the only rivers around here that flows north. Even when we aren't picking berries or catching frogs, the river is a great place for a dip on hot summer days.

Whatever berries the girls don't eat straight off the vine (and actually make it into their pails) usually end up swirled into ice cream, baked into a tart, blended into a smoothie, or simply served with dollops of whipped cream. If we are lucky enough to find elderberries, I'll cook them down into a syrup sweetened with a little Five Marys honey. A spoonful of elderberry syrup is known to keep your immune system strong

MY MOM'S RECIPE FOR AUTUMN apple crisp is a real treat that we all look forward to when the apples ripen on our trees. And because they all seem to come at once, it's excellent for making use of those fragrant apples before they go bad. We owe the delicious addition of the toasted pecans—a special Southern touch—to my sister, who lives in Nashville. This is an easy dessert to have kids help prep, as I remember doing often at my mom's side when I was little.

# JANNIE'S TOASTED PECAN–APPLE CRISP

*Makes 6 servings*

Preheat the oven to 375 degrees F. Grease an 8-inch square baking dish.

Peel and core the apples, then cut into ¾-inch chunks. Add to a large mixing bowl with the brown sugar, lemon juice, and ½ teaspoon of the cinnamon. Toss to combine, then spoon into the baking dish in an even layer.

In the same mixing bowl, stir together the oats, flour, sugar, pecans, remaining ½ teaspoon cinnamon, and the salt. Add the butter and vanilla and toss with a fork until the mixture is evenly moistened and clumpy.

Sprinkle the topping evenly over the apples. Bake until the topping is golden brown, the filling is bubbly, and the apples are tender when pierced with a paring knife, about 40 minutes. Let cool slightly before scooping into individual bowls. Serve each portion with a generous scoop of ice cream.

About 2½ pounds baking apples, such as Granny Smith, Gravenstein, Gala, or a combination
¼ cup packed light brown sugar
1 tablespoon freshly squeezed lemon juice
1 teaspoon ground cinnamon, divided
1 cup old-fashioned rolled oats
¾ cup all-purpose flour
⅔ cup granulated sugar
½ cup chopped toasted pecans
¼ teaspoon kosher salt
6 tablespoons unsalted butter, melted
½ teaspoon vanilla extract
Vanilla ice cream, for serving

THIS UNIQUE CUSTARD PIE ENCASES a decadent honey-almond filling in a crunchy oat-based pie shell. A sprinkle of flaky Maldon sea salt really brings out the subtle flavor of the almonds and beautifully showcases our own Five Marys honey. We often top it with big dollops of whipped cream, but a tart-sweet fruit compote, like sour cherry or blackberry, would also be at home alongside this dessert. I've always been a big fan of savory treats, and this pie is everything.

# SALTED HONEY-ALMOND PIE

*Makes 8 servings*

In a food processor, process the oats to a coarse meal. Add the flour, sugar, salt, and baking soda and process to combine. Add the butter and lard and pulse until the mixture resembles coarse fresh bread crumbs. Add the ice water and pulse a few times to bring the dough together. Dump the dough onto a clean work surface and press it together into a disk. Wrap tightly in plastic wrap, then refrigerate for at least 30 minutes or up to overnight. (The dough can then be frozen for up to 3 months.)

Unwrap the dough. On a lightly floured work surface (or between two sheets of parchment paper), using a rolling pin, roll out the dough to about ¼ inch thick. Gently ease the dough into a 9-inch pie pan. Trim the edge about 1 inch beyond the rim of the pan. The dough is delicate, but if it tears or has cracks, use the trimmings to patch and press it back together. Fold the dough edge underneath itself so it sits on the rim of the pie pan. Crimp the dough with your fingers or a fork. Freeze for at least 30 minutes.

To blind-bake the crust, preheat the oven to 375 degrees F. Line the pie dough with parchment and fill with dried beans or pie weights. Bake until the crust starts to lightly brown, about 20 minutes. Remove the weights and parchment and continue to bake until the crust looks dry, about 5 minutes.

Meanwhile, make the filling. In a food processor, process all of the ingredients until well combined.

When the crust is ready, reduce the oven temperature to 325 degrees F. Pour the filling into the hot crust and bake until the center is barely jiggly and the edges are set, 45 to 50 minutes.

Let the pie cool completely on a wire rack. Sprinkle with Maldon salt before slicing into wedges and serving with whipped cream.

**FOR THE CRUST**
1 cup old-fashioned rolled oats
1½ cups all-purpose flour
¼ cup packed light brown sugar
½ teaspoon kosher salt
¼ teaspoon baking soda
6 tablespoons unsalted butter
6 tablespoons lard, chilled
4 tablespoons ice-cold water

**FOR THE FILLING**
4 large whole eggs
4 large egg yolks
1 cup fine blanched almond flour
½ cup (1 stick) unsalted butter, at room temperature
½ cup honey
¼ cup packed light brown sugar
¼ cup heavy cream
1 tablespoon bourbon (optional)
1 teaspoon vanilla extract
¼ teaspoon baking powder
¼ teaspoon kosher salt

**FOR SERVING**
Maldon or other flaky sea salt
Whipped cream

# THE M5 PONY POSSE

We have a string of horses on the ranch. April "The Dream Pony" was our first and is Janie's horse. Despite being thirty-five years old, she is still spunky and will let just about anyone under a hundred pounds ride her. Domino—Maisie's horse—is a black-and-white beauty and a solid cow horse. Francie has two horses: Sunday, her drill-team horse, and Martin, her new rodeo horse she bought with her 4-H money. The biggest but gentlest horse in our string is Streak, Tess's twenty-two-year-old retired racehorse. (Don't tell Tess that "Streak" isn't the perfect name for her slow, steady horse or she's likely to burst into tears!) Stretch is my strong and trustworthy cow horse who takes me on trail rides with the girls and has taught me some new rodeo tricks.

And then there is Zippy. He's the most mischievous mini pony we've ever known and likes to sneak into the Camp kitchen any chance he can get. He is constantly looking for trouble, his hair sticks straight up, and he's always game for a selfie, all of which makes him the most endearing. The girls love trying to ride him (he likes to buck, but they don't fall very far), and he lives for treats, especially apples and sometimes even marshmallows or ice cream. Above all, he definitely brings big personality to our horse family!

MY PARENTS HAVE ALWAYS BEEN big entertainers and often hosted Friday night dinner parties when we were little. I have so many happy memories of my dad—known as Grampery to my girls—standing at the stove after dinner with his giant copper pot, whipping up his famous strawberry zabaglione and regaling his guests with jokes. This light and boozy custard dessert always felt so fancy, but it is a pretty simple dish to make. I love using our farm-fresh eggs because they add great color and flavor. Strawberries are always my dad's go-to since my great-grandfather farmed them, and it's worth seeking out the small fragrant ones, especially at the peak of their season. But sometimes I like to do a mix of berries depending on what is in season.

# GRAMPERY'S STRAWBERRY ZABAGLIONE

*Makes 6 to 8 servings*

Hull and quarter or slice the strawberries. In a large bowl, toss the berries with the 2 tablespoons sugar. Set aside for at least 10 minutes or up to 1 hour, stirring occasionally, until the sugar is dissolved. Divide half of the strawberries and their juices among six to eight dessert bowls.

In a medium mixing bowl, using an electric hand mixer or a whisk, beat the cream to medium-stiff peaks. Do not overbeat. Refrigerate until ready to use.

Fill a saucepan with about 1 inch of water and bring to a gentle simmer over medium-low heat. In a heatproof bowl that will fit snugly on top of the saucepan without touching the water, combine the egg yolks, vin santo, prosecco, and the remaining ½ cup sugar. Using a whisk or an electric hand mixer fitted with the whisk on medium-low speed, beat until the mixture is thick and frothy and reaches 150 to 155 degrees F on an instant-read thermometer, about 7 minutes.

Remove the bowl from the saucepan and continue to whisk until the mixture is lukewarm, about 5 minutes. Using a large silicone spatula, gently fold about one-third of the reserved whipped cream into the custard. Add the remaining whipped cream and gently fold it in until well combined.

Spoon the zabaglione over the strawberries, dividing it evenly among the bowls. Top with the remaining strawberries and their juices. Serve at once.

1½ pounds fresh strawberries
½ cup plus 2 tablespoons sugar, divided
¾ cup heavy cream
8 large egg yolks
⅓ cup vin santo or marsala
⅓ cup prosecco (or more vin santo or marsala)

STURDY AND RICH, THIS CROWD-PLEASING cake is ideal for a potluck or picnic. The chocolate chunks and fluffy cream cheese frosting distinguish it from everyday sweet bread. In fact, it's so good we convince ourselves it's basic banana bread and eat it any time of day. If you'd rather simplify this recipe, however, it can easily be transformed into just that. Omit the chocolate and frosting and divide the batter among greased loaf pans or lined muffin tins, and bake until a toothpick inserted into the center comes out clean (timing will vary). I like to bake two loaves and freeze one to pull out for weekend breakfast.

# BANANA CHOCOLATE CHUNK CAKE WITH CREAM CHEESE FROSTING

*Makes 8 to 10 servings*

Preheat the oven to 350 degrees F. Grease a 9-by-13-inch baking dish with cooking spray.

To make the cake, in the bowl of a stand mixer fitted with the paddle attachment or in a large mixing bowl using an electric hand mixer, beat together the butter and both sugars until smooth and creamy, about 2 minutes. Add the eggs, one at a time, beating well after each addition. Scrape down the sides of the bowl with a silicone spatula, then add the mashed bananas and vanilla. Beat until well combined.

In a medium bowl, whisk together the flour, baking powder, baking soda, cinnamon, and salt. Add half of the dry ingredients to the wet and mix on low speed until just combined, then add half the buttermilk and beat until combined. Add the remaining dry ingredients, then the remaining buttermilk, mixing until just combined. Add the chocolate chunks and mix on low speed until just combined.

Scrape the batter into the prepared pan. Bake until golden brown and a knife inserted into the center comes out clean, 50 to 60 minutes. Set aside to cool completely on a wire rack.

When the cake is cool, make the frosting. In the clean bowl of a stand mixer fitted with the whisk attachment or in a medium mixing bowl using an electric hand mixer, beat the cream cheese until smooth. Add the butter and vanilla and beat until well combined and smooth. Gradually add the powdered sugar in two or three steps, beating after each addition. Beat until the frosting is fluffy and smooth.

Spread a thick layer of frosting over the top of the cake. Cut into squares and serve.

**FOR THE CAKE**
1 cup (2 sticks) unsalted butter, at room temperature
1 cup packed light brown sugar
½ cup granulated sugar
3 large eggs
3 very ripe large bananas, mashed
2 teaspoons vanilla extract
3 cups all-purpose flour
1 teaspoon baking powder
1 teaspoon baking soda
1 teaspoon ground cinnamon
1 teaspoon kosher salt
1¼ cups well-shaken buttermilk
2 cups (about 10 ounces) semisweet chocolate chunks or chips

**FOR THE FROSTING**
1 (8-ounce) package cream cheese, at room temperature
½ cup (1 stick) unsalted butter, at room temperature
1 teaspoon vanilla extract
2½ cups powdered sugar, sifted

THICK SLICES OF SOFT, BUTTERY brioche add lightness and flavor to this warm and cozy dessert. Janie loves bread pudding nearly any way you serve it, but this lightly spiced version with dark butterscotch sauce (and plenty of whipped cream) is her top choice. You can leave out the bourbon, but I enjoy the sweet, deep flavor that our Five Marys bourbon contributes. In the winter, you can add sliced bananas to the pudding before baking, or serve the pudding with sliced ripe peaches or nectarines in the summer. It's a flexible and delectable treat and a great base to get creative with.

# BRIOCHE BREAD PUDDING <u>WITH</u> BOURBON-BUTTERSCOTCH SAUCE

*Makes 6 to 8 servings*

To make the bread pudding, grease a 9-by-13-inch baking dish with a generous amount of butter. In a large bowl, whisk together the milk, cream, eggs and yolks, sugar, vanilla, salt, and spices until well combined. Thickly slice the brioche, then cut or tear it into 1- to 2-inch pieces. Arrange the bread in the prepared pan in an even layer, then pour the milk mixture over it. Press the bread into the milk mixture. Set aside, pressing the bread down every so often, for 1 hour.

Preheat the oven to 325 degrees F. Bake the bread pudding until golden brown and cooked through, about 40 minutes. If you like it a bit darker, turn on the broiler to brown the top. Transfer to a wire rack to cool for 15 to 30 minutes, or cool to room temperature.

Meanwhile, make the sauce. In a medium saucepan over medium heat, melt the butter, then add the brown sugar, ⅓ cup of the cream, and the salt, stirring until smooth. Without stirring, but swirling the pan occasionally, let the mixture simmer for 4 minutes, or until the sugar melts and the mixture looks like caramel sauce (reduce the heat slightly if it starts to darken too quickly). Remove from the heat and stir in the remaining ⅓ cup cream, the bourbon, and the vanilla.

To serve, scoop the bread pudding into shallow bowls, then top with the butterscotch sauce and a dollop of whipped cream.

**FOR THE BREAD PUDDING**
Unsalted butter, for greasing the pan
1¾ cups whole milk
1 cup heavy cream
3 large whole eggs
5 large egg yolks
⅓ cup granulated sugar
2 teaspoons vanilla extract
½ teaspoon kosher salt
½ teaspoon ground cinnamon
¼ teaspoon ground allspice
¼ teaspoon ground ginger
1 (1-pound) loaf brioche or challah

**FOR THE SAUCE**
¼ cup unsalted butter
1½ cups packed light brown sugar
⅔ cup heavy cream, divided
½ teaspoon kosher salt
2 tablespoons bourbon
1 teaspoon vanilla extract

**FOR SERVING**
Whipped cream

# Acknowledgments

**T**HANK YOU!

On the ranch, we attribute most "wins" to a team effort . . . and this book was nothing short of that! I'm so proud of the compilation of *Ranch Raised* recipes and stories in this book.

A special thank-you to my friend and mentor Erin Benzakein of Floret Flower for pushing me to jump into the world of publishing and for holding my hand through the process. Erin is a champion of positivity to me and so many other women in small business; I am so grateful for her friendship and her encouragement and for her being the very first to spark this cookbook to life.

Thank you to my wonderful agent, Leslie Stoker, who took the first glimmer of my idea in a homemade proposal, believed in it, and helped launch it from the start. And for being a continued source of advice and a beacon of navigation in my first foray into publishing.

A giant thank-you to my recipe developer and coauthor, Kim Laidlaw, who became a good friend after a winter weekend on the ranch with our families two years ago and who put a huge effort into this book. We spent many hours over hot tea, ranch breakfasts, sidecars, and emails. Kim gets my style and makes beautiful food, and she was a wizard at transforming my favorite dishes into tried-and-true recipes to share with home cooks.

A huge thanks to my publishing team at Sasquatch Books, especially executive editor Susan Roxborough, who became an "insta-friend" long before we signed this book. Susan had big dreams for this book before I did and was instrumental in bringing it to life in such a beautiful way. I'm so thankful insta-friendship turned into a true friendship as a result. Thank you also to art director Anna Goldstein, marketing director Nikki Sprinkle, VP of sales and strategy Jenny Abrami, senior production editor Jill Saginario, copyeditor Rachelle Longé McGhee, and the whole crew at Sasquatch.

The stunning photography was also a team effort. My longtime friend Kathryn Gamble, who shot all the gorgeous landscapes and lifestyle photography of our family, has been to the ranch every year we've lived here. She captures the magic of ranch life by riding and living alongside us. Kathryn has seen its progression and how our family has grown with it, and for that perspective and friendship I am so thankful! A big thanks to food photographer Charity Burggraaf and food stylist Nathan Carrabba, who captured the deliciousness of the recipes and kept smiling even when our horses invaded the outdoor Camp kitchen and ate half of our fresh produce and flowers from the garden. (A special thanks to the entire team for enduring our sneaky miniature pony Zippy, who loved to steal treats from the kitchen any chance he got!)

I am grateful for my family, where all of the inspiration for these *Ranch Raised* recipes come from. I am especially thankful for my parents, Janet and John, who gave me a foundation for entertaining; my husband, Brian, who appreciates everything I put on the table and loves to cook right alongside me; my sister, Ann, who brings her Southern inspiration and shares my love for all big dreams; and my sister-in-law Katherine, who always inspires me with great ideas in the kitchen or at the bar.

Most of all, thank you to my four little Marys, who put up with many long days and nights recipe testing and taking photos and editing this book. They were good sports to take time away from their horses and barefoot summer to get a little primped for Mom's cookbook shoots!

And last but not least, my faithful dog Dixie, who sat at my feet for every word written and every scrap shared while cooking *Ranch Raised* recipes in my kitchen.

# Index

# About the Author

**MARY HEFFERNAN** and her husband, Brian, left behind the busy life they'd built in Silicon Valley to become cattle ranchers with their four young daughters—all named Mary. Together they own and operate Five Marys Farms, an 1,800-acre ranch in the mountains of Northern California where they live, work, and raise all-natural beef, pork, and lamb. Mary and Brian sell and ship directly from the farm to families all over the US through their Farm Store in Fort Jones. They share their meats with local customers and visitors from far and wide at their popular restaurant and bar, Five Marys Burgerhouse. Five Marys was awarded Best Farm in America by *Paleo* magazine and has been featured in *Oprah* magazine, *Real Simple*, *Sunset*, and other national publications. She has also appeared on *Today*. Mary has a fiercely loyal following on social media and hosts popular summer farm dinners and weekend retreats at the ranch with cooking, cocktails, and butchery classes. She and Brian believe in raising meat naturally and that great cooking starts with well-raised ingredients.

# *Contributors*

**KIM LAIDLAW**, owner of Cast Iron Media, LLC, is an award-winning cookbook editor, recipe developer, and the author of five cookbooks. With more than twenty years of experience in cookbook publishing, Kim has managed hundreds of projects from conception to completion. Her clients include Weber, Kendall-Jackson, Williams Sonoma, KitchenAid, *Saveur*, American Girl, *EatingWell*, and more. Kim is a recipe developer and tester for high-profile brands, chefs, and cookbook authors. She is a former instructor at the San Francisco Cooking School, and has worked as a professional baker. Kim lives in Petaluma, California, with her husband, their daughter, and a bountiful home garden.

**CHARITY BURGGRAAF** specializes in food photography. Her work has appeared in *Bon Appétit*, *Food & Wine*, *Saveur*, the *New York Times*, *LA Times*, *Vogue*, and *Travel + Leisure*. She has photographed over two dozen cookbooks, most notably The Willows Inn's *Sea and Smoke* and *Lummi: Island Cooking*. When not shooting, she can be found throwing pottery or gardening with her kitty, Hazel.

**KATHRYN GAMBLE** was born in Chicago, raised in Atlanta, and lived in New York City before moving to Iowa. She studied at the International Center of Photography in New York and earned her BA in journalism from the University of Georgia. A selection of her commercial photography clients include the ACLU, Meredith Corporation, *Sweet Paul* magazine, *Better Homes & Gardens*, Pratt Institute, The Cooper Union, and Von Maur. She is a regular contributor to the *New York Times*. Kathryn is the photographer of *Women and the Land*, a book about twenty-six women farmers in Iowa, and it is her first book. She is married to Rick Lozier, who is also a commercial photographer. They have a studio together, as well as two sons, Jackson and Walker.

# Conversions

| VOLUME | | | LENGTH | | WEIGHT | |
|---|---|---|---|---|---|---|
| UNITED STATES | METRIC | IMPERIAL | UNITED STATES | METRIC | AVOIRDUPOIS | METRIC |
| ¼ tsp. | 1.25 mL | | ⅛ in. | 3 mm | ¼ oz. | 7 g |
| ½ tsp. | 2.5 mL | | ¼ in. | 6 mm | ½ oz. | 15 g |
| 1 tsp. | 5 mL | | ½ in. | 1.25 cm | 1 oz. | 30 g |
| ½ Tbsp. | 7.5 mL | | 1 in. | 2.5 cm | 2 oz. | 60 g |
| 1 Tbsp. | 15 mL | | 1 ft. | 30 cm | 3 oz. | 90 g |
| ⅛ c. | 30 mL | 1 fl. oz. | | | 4 oz. | 115 g |
| ¼ c. | 60 mL | 2 fl. oz. | | | 5 oz. | 150 g |
| ⅓ c. | 80 mL | 2.5 fl. oz. | | | 6 oz. | 175 g |
| ½ c. | 125 mL | 4 fl. oz. | | | 7 oz. | 200 g |
| 1 c. | 250 mL | 8 fl. oz. | | | 8 oz. (½ lb.) | 225 g |
| 2 c. (1 pt.) | 500 mL | 16 fl. oz. | | | 9 oz. | 250 g |
| 1 qt. | 1 L | 32 fl. oz. | | | 10 oz. | 300 g |

| TEMPERATURE | | | | WEIGHT (cont.) | |
|---|---|---|---|---|---|
| | | | | 11 oz. | 325 g |
| OVEN MARK | FAHRENHEIT | CELSIUS | GAS | 12 oz. | 350 g |
| Very cool | 250–275 | 130–140 | ½–1 | 13 oz. | 375 g |
| Cool | 300 | 150 | 2 | 14 oz. | 400 g |
| Warm | 325 | 165 | 3 | 15 oz. | 425 g |
| Moderate | 350 | 175 | 4 | 16 oz. (1 lb.) | 450 g |
| Moderately hot | 375 | 190 | 5 | 1½ lb. | 750 g |
| Fairly hot | 400 | 200 | 6 | 2 lb. | 900 g |
| Hot | 425 | 220 | 7 | 2¼ lb. | 1 kg |
| Very hot | 450 | 230 | 8 | 3 lb. | 1.4 kg |
| Very hot | 475 | 245 | 9 | 4 lb. | 1.8 kg |

For ease of use, conversions have been rounded.

Printed in China

SASQUATCH BOOKS with colophon is a registered trademark of Penguin Random House LLC

24 23 22 21 20          9 8 7 6 5 4 3 2 1

Editor: Susan Roxborough | Production editor: Jill Saginario

Cover and food photographer: Charity Burggraaf (pages 14–15, 19–20, 23, 28–30, 34–35, 37–38, 41, 43–45, 49–50, 53, 56, 59–60, 62, 65–66, 68, 74–75, 78–80, 82, 86, 88, 91–93, 95, 97, 101–104, 108, 112, 116–118, 121, 125–129, 132, 136, 138, 142, 144, 146, 152, 156, 159, 164, 166, 169, 172, 175–176, 179, 181–183, 187–188, 190, 192, 195–196, 199, 203, 205–206, 209–210, 212–214, 217–218, 221, 227–229, 232, 236–237, 239, 242, 245, 251–252, 255)

Lifestyle photographer: Kathryn Gamble (pages i–13, 16, 18, 25, 31, 36, 46, 54–55, 70–73, 76, 84–85, 98–99, 107, 111, 122, 130, 137, 143, 149–151, 154–155, 160–162, 170–171, 177, 184, 202, 222–223, 240–241, 246–249, 256–257, 260, 266–268, 270, 272–275)

Food stylist: Nathan Carrabba | Designer: Anna Goldstein

Library of Congress Cataloging-in-Publication Data
Names: Heffernan, Mary, 1978- author. | Laidlaw, Kim, author.
Title: Five Marys ranch raised cookbook : homegrown recipes from our family to yours / by Mary Heffernan with Kim Laidlaw.
Identifiers: LCCN 2020003111 (print) | LCCN 2020003112 (ebook) | ISBN 9781632173072 (hardcover) | ISBN 9781632173089 (ebook)
Subjects: LCSH: Cooking, American. | Ranch life—California. | LCGFT: Cookbooks.
Classification: LCC TX715 .H3995 2020 (print) | LCC TX715 (ebook) | DDC 641.59794—dc23
LC record available at https://lccn.loc.gov/2020003111
LC ebook record available at https://lccn.loc.gov/2020003112

ISBN: 978-1-63217-307-2

Sasquatch Books | 1904 Third Avenue, Suite 710 | Seattle, WA 98101

SasquatchBooks.com